ASCENSION
THROUGH ORBS

ASCENSION
THROUGH ORBS

by
Diana Cooper & Kathy Crosswell

FINDHORN PRESS

© Diana Cooper and Kathy Crosswell 2009

First published by Findhorn Press 2009

ISBN 978-1-84409-150-8

British Library Cataloguing-in-Publication Data.
A catalogue record for this book is available from the British Library.

Edited by Michael Hawkins
Cover design by Guter Punkt & Thierry Bogliolo
Interior design by Prepress-Solutions.com
Printed in the European Union

3 4 5 6 7 8 9 10 11 12 13 14 15 14 13 12 11 10

Published by
Findhorn Press
117–121 High Street,
Forres IV36 1AB
Scotland, UK

t +44(0)1309 690582
f +44(0)131 777 2711
e info@findhornpress.com
www.findhornpress.com

Dedications and Acknowledgements

Diana would like to dedicate this book to the ascension of the planet and everyone on it.

Kathy would like to dedicate this book to her mum and dad, husband Paul and her children Emily, Blake and Harry, whom she adores.

We would like to thank the following contributors for kindly allowing us to use their Orb pictures in this book, as well as those who have sent us Orbs which we have not been able to use here:

Lesley Whitehead
Joyce Rimmell
Kathy Smith
Julie Kingsley
Noel O'Neill
Pam Raworth
Einav Adir
Mandy Whalley
Patti McCullough
Eugene McGill
Tammie Stair

Banita Kern
Kari Palmgren
Ann-Marie Bentham
Outi Seppi
Dawn Gilroy Smith
Gillian Barnes
Alec Turner
Ingrid Jorgensen
Eugenie Moreton
Audrey and Stuart Mackie
Jennifer Coombes

Table of Contents

Section 3 – The Ascended Masters

Section 4 – Nature, Animals, Stars

Introduction

How Kathy and I were brought together

In November 2007 I was finishing *The Wonder of Unicorns* and anticipating a much overdue rest. Some friends suggested that I should write about Orbs which were coming to the fore. I replied that I was not interested in Orbs and had received no guidance to do anything with them. Exactly one week later Kathy Crosswell came to my house. She is a medium and spiritual teacher, so we chatted about many things. All at once we noticed the candle starting to flicker wildly. We looked at each other and said simultaneously, 'Spirit has a message for us.'

My guide, Kumeka, and her guide, Wywyvsil, connected with us immediately. They indicated that they had brought us together to write about Orbs which are very important for the ascension of the planet. They told us that either of us could take the project forward but when we linked together we could reach a higher frequency. That was why they wanted us to write books jointly. They also informed us that we had been genetic sisters and had worked together in Golden Atlantis.

My exhaustion was forgotten. For six months Kathy and I met twice a week, while the angels poured energy through us, which we both experienced. It was exhilarating and exciting. During this time many guides and angels worked with us and taught us about Orbs. We looked at thousands that were sent to us and learnt how to differentiate them. First we wrote *Enlightenment Through Orbs – The Awesome Truth Revealed,* which offers introductory information and takes you on a journey of awakening. Our guides and angels gave us that title and were clear that was it! No sooner had we finished it than they asked us to start immediately on this book, *Ascension Through Orbs.*

Orbs offer keys to higher consciousness to accelerate our ascension. Because there are waves of ascension now starting they wanted this book to be available to facilitate and boost this possibility for as many of you as possible.

Kathy and I work in a different but complementary way. I look at the Orb photographs and ask questions. My mind goes into silence and the answer comes into it. Kathy, being clairsentient and a medium receives the same responses in a different way. She can also enter the Orbs to access cosmic information from them. We work well together and writing this book has been very exciting for both of us.

They have opened up a new world to us and we humbly share their information in *Ascension Through Orbs,* knowing that we still have an enormous amount to learn.

We hope that you feel the awe just as we did as the Orbs awaken you to their messages.

Taking photographs of Orbs

Orbs respond to the consciousness of the photographer. If your heart is open and you resonate at a fifth dimensional frequency you can take Orb photographs.

Orbs are everywhere, day and night, but are more easily filmed at night in the rain! Having so said, we have both taken many beautiful Orbs in the day and have been sent hundreds of them.

Why not use a digital camera, open your heart, call in the angels, start clicking and see what happens? It is most exciting to go out into my garden at night and click away on my camera. There are always Orbs! Sometimes there are just spirits passing through but if it is windy or raining there are often crowds of tiny fairies, protected by angels of love. These cluster round the trees and certain bushes.

I am delighted at the number of archangels who visit my home and the unicorns who shine their light into my garden.

What Ascension Through Orbs offers

When I updated *A New Light on Ascension* to include the latest information available, it was a foundation for ascension, which still holds true. In this book I expand this by providing new and exciting in-depth material about the twelve chakras, which will help your spiritual energy centres to evolve. I add up to date news about the spiritual hierarchy and the most advanced energies available to assist your own journey, as well as meditations and exercises. **Most important of all we show you certain Orbs which will accelerate your spiritual growth and ascension. Every Orb in this book offers an activation and access to higher energies.**

But I think the most exciting new development for this book has been the ascended masters who are showing themselves. These are the great beings we are trying to emulate, those who have walked the ascension path before us. As we look at them in their angel Orbs, we can absorb their light and wisdom, and this assists our spiritual growth very much. We have published some of their pictures in *Ascension Through Orbs* and I hope you will enjoy looking at their faces, learning about them and expanding your consciousness through them.

The more people who ascend the easier it is for others to follow in their footsteps. At this time many wise beings have reincarnated to walk with us and show us the way. It may be that you are one of them.

This book will open you up to who you truly are, so that you can be a light bearer to lead others up the spiritual mountain to ascension.

It feels as if this series of Orb books, which Kathy and I are writing, is a team effort, you, us and the spiritual hierarchy. We could not do it without all of you who have sent in your Orb photographs and generously allowed us to use them. I have spent hours examining every one of them and learning from them. Our guides and angels have also been part of the team, for Kumeka, Archangel Michael and Mother Mary have been particularly involved in giving us explanations and information and expanding our consciousness.

There is currently a massive movement on the part of the spiritual hierarchy to help the ascension of the planet and everyone on her. The Orbs are a huge part of this, so please awaken and expand your mind and allow them to take you to higher levels of awareness and ascension.

When Kathy and I wrote *Enlightenment Through Orbs – The Awesome Truth Revealed,* we felt we were being taken on an extraordinary consciousness expanding experience. Nothing would seem the same again. However, *Ascension Through Orbs* has extended and solidified this. Once more we have been offered wonderful explanations by Mother Mary, Kumeka, Archangels Michael, Raphael, Roquiel and Uriel, the Seraphim Seraphina and Wywyvsil, a Lord of Karma, which have not just added to our knowledge but made sense of a wider spectrum of universal truth. There is only one thing we can say to the Spiritual Hierarchy and that is, 'Thank you.'

Ascension Through Orbs offers a right brain experience, so please read it with your heart not your head.

Section One

Ascension – An Overview

Chapter One

Ascension Through Orbs

What is Ascension?

Ascension is the bringing down of light from Source through your Monad into the cells of your body until they are so saturated that they can no longer hold the divine vibration while remaining physical. There are many levels of ascension. The ultimate one is where your physical body dissolves in the light and you take it with you into the higher realms. This is a very rare choice for the soul because of the impact on loved ones and the fear it sometimes engenders. Most evolved people choose to die naturally and ascend as they pass over.

What if you are almost ready for ascension when you pass over but have not quite reached the light levels required?

If you pass just before your light levels reach that needed for ascension, masters and angels on the other side help you to attain the required light quotient. We were sent a wonderful Orb picture which demonstrated beautifully the amount of help available to you if you are almost, but not quite ready.

In the picture there were two Orbs, the lower faint one being the spirit of a woman, who had just died and was almost at the point of ascending. However, she had not quite reached the frequency enabling her to ascend fully. If she had been absolutely ready many archangels would have collected her. Instead you could see in the upper Orb that three angels of love and Kumeka had come for her bringing her child who passed before her. The child was meeting her mother to encourage her to ascend. It was a reminder that there is so much spiritual help available.

Does looking at Orbs help your light quotient for ascension?

Certain ones, yes. All the Orbs in this book raise your light levels if you look at them and meditate with them. We offer you meditations which will help you even more.

Can you ascend if you still have karma?

In order to ascend you must have balanced your karma. There are divine dispensations currently on offer, so if you feel you have some karma remaining, ask the Lords of Karma to help you release it when you meditate.

Will you re-incarnate if you have ascended?

Many who have ascended choose to come back in service. In this case their soul will often select a family in which they undertake family karma and they may face very challenging conditions.

Spiritual practises for ascension

Chanting

Hymns, Sanskrit chants, Buddhist chants, bahjans and native spiritual chants all have an effect on your aura, especially when your intention and focus is pure.

Prayer

The intention and dedication of the prayer is important. Be centred, clear and passionate, asking for the highest good. Mechanical prayer by rote is not effective for ascension. We were sent the most magnificent Orb by a lady who had been saying her prayers. The Orb, which was her Guardian Angel, was radiant and pure white. It had been expanded by her prayers and had spread out of her room and over her car in the drive. It was taking the energy of her prayers to her soul, partly for her soul's use and partly for the world. It visibly demonstrated the power of prayer!

Meditation

Taking quiet time for contemplation or meditation is an important spiritual practice.

Service

Service work with love and joy in your heart raises your light levels. It is fine to be paid for it as this keeps the karma balanced and you have to live – but give with an open heart.

Devotion

Whatever you do, do with devotion and gratitude. Whether it is gardening, teaching children to swim or being a driving instructor, dedicate your work to God and be grateful for everything you experience. If you go for a walk set an intention that will raise your frequency. It may be a gratitude walk, where you give thanks for everything you can think of. You might dedicate a car journey to love, so during the drive you think all the loving things you can about a person or situation.

Yoga

This calms the mind, releases toxins from the body, clears particular nadirs and prepares you for meditation.

Spiritual reading

Reading spiritual books opens you to higher possibilities.

Spiritual conversation

When you talk about the great saints and masters, the spiritual hierarchy and the divine energies available and waiting to be accessed, you are illuminated with their light.

Dedicating your sleep time

Every night your spirit leaves your body and journeys during your sleep. Where you go depends on several factors.

If your soul has dedicated you to healing, your spirit will visit the spirits of the sick or bereaved to offer them healing or comfort. You may find people tell you that you came into their dream and helped them, so if you feel this is part of your service work, do it willingly and ask for help and protection.

You may do rescue work in the inner planes, helping stuck souls to pass over. This is particularly taxing if there has been a disaster and many spirits need your assistance. Again do it willingly, offer your help and ask to be guided and protected.

You may visit the teaching temples in the inner planes, or the seats of the ascended masters or archangels to learn or to increase your light levels. If you want to do this read about them, focus on them and before you go to sleep ask to be taken there. In this book we give you a list of those retreats of masters and archangels which are particularly important for ascension. Orb (1) will also assist you by offering an invitation which will be received by your soul.

Masters travelling to the Seventh Heaven:
Mary Magdelene, El Morya and Serapis Bey

At the top right of picture (1) the white Orb with wings is Mary Magdelene radiating heart energy. The two Orbs together at the top and one right at the bottom are aspects of El Morya and the two at the bottom are aspects of Serapis Bey. They

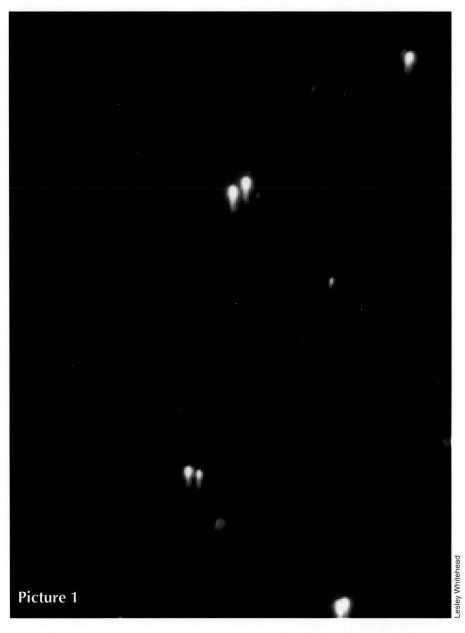

Picture 1

Lesley Whitehead

are on their way to the Seventh Heaven for a meeting where the angels and masters are taught by God. The blue orbs are Kumeka's angels protecting them.

When you look at picture (1) you receive an invitation to the Seventh Heaven

Attitude

There are many things which release the old and open you to the possibility of something higher and greater. Make sure that your attitude and intent is aligned to ascension as you do them, for example, horse riding, swimming, writing or creative work.

Chapter Two

Psychic Protection

As soon as you open up spiritually your light can be seen by those who would like to steal some of your high frequency energy.

Do you need psychic protection?

This is one of the questions I am most commonly asked. Many people feel that they don't need protection for there is nothing to be protected against. However, we do live in a plane of duality and for everything in the light, there is an equivalent in the dark, so there are beings of lower intent around us. In fact the more light you radiate, the more moths are drawn towards you.

Your aura is your electromagnetic shield which guards your energy centres. If negative energies or entities get into your aura because it is open, they can affect you, sometimes profoundly, so that they block your ascension.

If you are very grounded, masculine orientated, closed, practical, down to earth and unimaginative, you will need less protection than the person who is ungrounded, open, psychic, sensitive and feminine orientated.

Certain things can open your aura up, like shock, fear, excitement, bereavement, psychic or spiritual work and some drugs. Also when you walk in nature, you relax and open yourself up to the healing it offers.

When should you protect yourself?

It is sensible to put on psychic protection when you get up in the morning, before you go to bed, when you meditate or do your spiritual practice and if you are entering a place where the energies are questionable or there are lots of spirits about.

We were sent a picture of someone who had been to visit the grave of a loved one. Cemeteries are gathering places for spirits and she was completely surrounded by hundreds who had not passed over, all looking to her for help. She was unaware of this and if her aura was open and unprotected, they could pour their fear, desperation, longings, addictions or any other lower feelings into her. She would not know why she was feeling sick, depressed or anxious. She might say, 'Whenever I visit Dad's grave I feel terrible for days afterwards,' little knowing that needy spirits had compromised and drawn on her energy.

How can you protect yourself?

The most important thing to remember is that your intent and focus affect the efficacy of your protection.

Secondly, anything that you believe in, consciously or unconsciously will protect you. If you had a past life connected to Jesus or a Christian religious life, you will find the Christ light to be very protective. If you are very linked to Archangel Michael or Archangel Gabriel, you will find their cloaks to be powerful. Those with strong Egyptian links will be drawn to a pyramid. You may like to use more than one protection as your past life experiences will affect your beliefs, without your necessarily being aware of the impact. Below are some potent ways of protecting yourself and your family:

1. Archangel Michael's cloak

Archangel Michael is the angel of protection. He holds a Sword of Truth and a Shield of Protection as he fights for those who need him. He also wears a deep blue cloak and when his angels place this round you, it will enclose your aura.

It adds to the energy of prayer if you hold your hands in the prayer position. So does lighting a candle.

Quietly ask Archangel Michael to enfold you in his deep blue cloak of protection. Wait a moment and you may feel his angels placing it over you. If you don't sense this, visualise the cloak going over you. Mentally zip it up from your feet to your chin and pull the hood up over your crown and third eye.

Then trust that you are protected.

2. Archangel Gabriel's reflective ball

Call on Archangel Gabriel to place his pure white reflective ball around you so that any lower energies bounce off it, leaving you protected.

3. The Gold Ray of Christ

This is an extremely powerful protection. Invoke the gold ray of Christ three times, like this. 'I now invoke the gold ray of Christ for my total protection.' X 3. Then say, 'It is done. I am protected in the Christ light.'

The Christ light is totally protective, so if you are pure enough to live in it at all times, you are completely safe. However there is no one currently in incarnation who has that level of purity.

4. The symbol of a cross

This is another very powerful symbol, which has the force of the Christ energy behind it. Visualise a cross in front of you, one behind you, another to the left and one to the right of you, one above and one below you. This will effectively seal your aura.

For some people it is very important to do something physical. In that case, with your finger, draw a cross above or in front of each of your chakras, mentally imagining them sealed and protected.

5. The Godforce

If you strongly believe in Source or God, call on the power to protect you and visualise it doing so in whatever form is comfortable for you.

6. Mirrors

This is an immensely effective way of repelling psychic attack. Anyone who is sending you angry, malicious or destructive thoughts is directing their energy towards you in such a way that this can pierce your aura.

You may feel drained of energy, irritable, nervous or ill with no idea why. When the force they are sending towards you hits the mirror, it is reflected back to them. Some people do not think this is spiritual but it does offer the other person instant karma and an opportunity to grow.

Ask that a mirror, facing outward be placed between you and the source of attack for the highest good of all concerned. Then visualise mirrors on every side of you, so that arrows are deflected back to where they came.

7. Prayers

Certain prayers like The Lord's Prayer or the Gayatri mantra protect you.

How can you protect children?

Most children are open and vulnerable. Often the masculine energy of their father or an uncle or grandfather will automatically protect them. However, if they do not have a strong male parent or relative they will need extra protection.

Pray for protection for the child and specifically ask for that which you feel will be most helpful. Then visualise it surrounding the child.

Many of the new children are psychic, open and ungrounded and they can be helped if you also seal their auras physically. In that case rub your hands together to create energy. Hold them up and ask the angels of protection or Archangel Michael to touch them. Then run your palms over the child's aura, about 4″ (10cms) away from their body until you feel their aura has become even and is sealed.

If you place a photo of the child on Orb (22) of Archangel Michael (Chapter 15) they will automatically receive his protection.

Chapter Three

Life Choices for Ascension

Is purification important for ascension?

Your aura is like a sponge which absorbs everything around you. If you leave a sponge in filthy water, you expect it to be dirty. If you leave it in clear, clean water, you will squeeze out clear liquid. You live in the equivalent of a pool of your thoughts and emotions. It is also affected by everything and everyone around you, from the television you watch to the people you mix with. What is your pool like?

An analogy for purification and ascension

Imagine you are a beautiful pure white cloth that has been dunked in the dirt. The mud may be ingrained or it may just be superficial. If your soul is ingrained with negativity, there will be much purification needed. If it is just superficial you will simply need to keep yourself cleansed.

When the cloth is washed and sparkling white, you hang it out to dry in the sunshine where it takes in the light. If the conditions are inclement this might take a long time. On the other hand, if it is a sunny day this process will take an instant. Your soul dictates the conditions around you, and you decide how to handle them.

One person may rush outside to hold out the cloth to the wind and any available sun. Another may say it's not worth it, so does not take the opportunities presented for spiritual growth.

When you are laid out pure and shining on the table your purpose has been accomplished.

Reading this book and looking at the Orbs is one such opportunity that you have attracted.

Life choices for ascension

1. Television

Choose with discernment what television you watch. One low frequency programme can fill you up with heavy vibrations whereas a programme of light and laughter can shake out the old and lift you.

2. Reading

Choose your reading matter carefully. A spiritual book radiates light into the room and at the same time raises your frequency as you read it.

3. Flowers

Do not underestimate the power of flowers. They are not just beautiful. They purify the atmosphere, raise the frequency, give you healing and can help you in many ways. Plant them if you can. Buy them for your living space and make sure you bless them and thank them.

Diana's story. I was supposed to be taking a seminar abroad but had heard nothing from the promoter, who, I subsequently learnt, had a breakdown and was in hospital. Calls and e-mails from my office were ignored. I did not even know where to go. But I was concerned about anyone who may have booked for the event and I guess this opened a chink in my aura.

On the day when I should have been flying to the workshop, I went for a walk in the countryside. A forsythia bush, covered in yellow flowers, was growing all by itself and I moved up to it. When I was about three feet (one metre) away from it, a bright yellow light suddenly streamed out of it into my aura. I jumped in surprise. Archangel Michael said that the would-be promoter was sending me anger and my concern had opened me up to it. To help me the archangel had led me to the bush of yellow flowers which sent their energy to empower my solar plexus. Flowers are amazing energy healers.

4. Friends

Select your friends and companions with circumspection. Those people who are depressed, envious, gossip, indulge in addictions or are of unpleasant disposition are better avoided. You may be able to raise their frequency but it is easy to let them bring you down. If you are truly aiming for ascension it would serve your spiritual growth to walk alone rather than spend time with undesirable people. During your period alone you can raise your consciousness so that you attract in new friends who are aligned to your higher wavelength.

5. Holidays

There are many life enhancing places to visit, where you can relax and recharge yourself. We were sent some photographs of girls who were on a drinking gambling holiday in Las Vegas. They were in a casino full of entities and low vibrations. Yet they were clearly of a high frequency for huge unicorn orbs had wrapped round them and were protecting them. It was clear that it did not serve their ascension process to be in there.

Fifth dimensional people often prefer to spend their leisure time in a pursuit that will raise their frequency. Mountains, sea air, countryside, exercise, swimming with dolphins, visiting an ashram or inspiring friends will make your aura glow and sparkle.

Some use their spare time in service, visiting prisons or helping those in need, and they will need protection.

6. Hobbies

If your hobbies no longer enthuse you, find new ones. Those that fascinate you and cause you to meet fellow enthusiasts who light you up, are perfect. Choose pastimes that endow you with feelings of peace, exhilaration, serenity, caring, loving, fun or any positive qualities. If they involve service and you enjoy it, that also assists ascension.

7. Being in nature

Gardening or walking is a wonderful way to light up your cells and connect to Mother Earth, especially if you have time to enjoy the views and birds, animals, flowers and all the life that is around you. Hug a tree. Bless the flowers and the waters.

8. Exercise

Healthy exercise produces more endorphins and makes your light glow more brightly.

9. Laughter

Laughter illuminates your aura. The more you laugh the lighter you become. It shakes out the heavier vibrations and opens you to more divine energy.

10. Water

Showers, baths, swimming, paddling, having fun in the water, all cleanse your aura. Swimming in clear water has a very purifying effect!

11. Fire

At the time of writing I feel very blessed to have a wood burning stove in my kitchen. I can sit and watch the flames and know that my fire is offering much more than warmth.

12. Beautiful and sacred objects

Surround yourself with beautiful things filled with sacred energy and they will radiate light into your environment.

13. Music

Devotional, inspirational, energy raising, harmonious music can purify and light up your aura.

14. Creative expression

Drawing, painting, making paper flowers, creating jewellery or sacred dancing purifies your energy and opens your heart.

15. Playing with animals and children

Innocence or being in your essence is an important quality for ascension, and playing with animals or children opens your heart to this.

16. Setting your friends, family and loved ones free

When you are corded to another, you hold onto them. In order to ascend and let your loved ones walk their highest spiritual path, set them free. This does not mean that you love them less but that you love them in a much higher way, without neediness or expectation.

We were sent Photo (2) by Joyce Rimmell, which was taken when she was invited by her grandson to go to his passing out parade for the RAF, and it gave her much reassurance. She said, 'It would be a good one to help to explain that the angels and loved ones are everywhere even in places where the energy feels so negative.' Indeed she is right and there is much more. The big Orb contains unicorn energy and an angel of love.

The angel of love is helping all the people to cooperate and work together for the common good, while the unicorn is helping families to release their loved ones for a higher purpose. Above her grandson's head is his guardian angel with the spirit of a loved one who has come to visit. The other officers also have their guardian angels above them. The other Orb at the front and Orbs above the men on the parade are spirits of friends, relatives and other loved ones coming with their angels to watch the parade!

Picture 2

Joyce Rimell

A unicorn and an angel of love

When you look at photo (2) you receive angelic assistance to help you set your loved ones free.

***

Picture 3

Kathy Smith

17. On the ascension pathway it is most important to be yourself.

In picture (3) angels of Archangels Uriel and Raphael have come into an office where an eighteenth birthday is being celebrated. The angels have brought spirits of loved ones, who have passed, with them. In this photograph you can clearly see the guardian angel of the lady on the bottom right, protecting her. The lady in green has the huge Orb of angels of Archangels Uriel and Raphael behind her, which has come to help all the people feel good. Archangel Uriel's angel is offering everyone in the office a sense of assurance about who they are and Archangel Raphael's is radiating a feeling of prosperity to them. The spirits are bringing the message that there is a higher way of doing things and a reminder that there is a world beyond work.

Angels of Archangels Uriel and Raphael

When you look at Orb (3) you receive permission to be yourself wherever you are, so that you can walk the ascension pathway as yourself.

***

Picture 4

Julie Kingsley

18. Family Life.

One of the greatest spiritual responsibilities that most people undertake in a lifetime is the bringing up of their children. They are souls entrusted to their care.

In picture (4) the Orb is actively radiating and you can tell this by the shape. It is Archangel Michael with a unicorn and the guardian angel of the mother. Archangel Michael is protecting the whole family, while the unicorn energy is bringing enlightenment to them all. The mother's guardian angel is holding her light steady.

In this happy family picture the Orb is sending energy to the woman to protect her throat chakra and enable her to rise to the fifth dimension.

The Orb has placed itself in the crown of the innocent girl because she is unconsciously linking in to keep her mother in a space of childlike innocence and purity for ascension.

The Orb is also holding the whole family in the right energy for ascension.

Archangel Michael with a unicorn and guardian angel

When you look at picture (4) it activates enlightenment that takes you on your path to ascension.

***

Orb (5) also illustrates the importance of family life and how much the archangels are helping to bring whole families to ascension. This picture contains an Orb of angels of Archangels Uriel, Raphael and Zadkiel with spirits. It brings great promise for Archangel Uriel is actively taking out energy that would limit this family, so they can all move onto an ascension pathway. Archangel Zadkiel is pouring in joy and transmutation, while Archangel Raphael is holding them all in healing light. The spirits are training to become guides and are learning what holds people back from ascension.

Angels of Archangels Uriel, Raphael and Zadkiel and spirits help a family

When you look at picture (5) you receive a clearance of your consciousness that will enable you to move out of your limited space onto an ascension path.

Picture 5

Noel O'Neill

Chapter Four

Spirit Guides

You only have one Guardian Angel who is allocated to you for your lifetime but you have many spirit guides. They are attracted to you according to the level of light you radiate, so as you become more enlightened, higher guides work with you, until you may even have an ascended master by your side.

You may have several guides with you at a time. One might help you with your financial issues. Another may have been a nun, who enables you to feel calm or guide you spiritually. A third may be assisting you in your business. A fourth is perhaps a very wise ancient. Your thoughts draw them in so they will respond to your needs and also to your requests.

In order to become a spirit guide you go through extensive training in the inner planes, for it is a highly responsible position. However, those who have loved you may also help you. They are helpers in spirit but not guides.

Many spirit guides present themselves as they were in their last incarnation. As these had to be lives of wisdom in order for them to qualify, they are often Native American Indians or monks or doctors.

Kumeka

Guides have usually had a physical incarnation. My chief guide, Kumeka, however has never lived on Earth. He is a higher master, drawn to this planet from another universe to help in these times.

Lone Wolf

I was most intrigued when we were sent picture (6), for the Orb turned out to contain Pam Raworth's grandmother with Lone Wolf, a well known and popular guide. We learnt that Lone Wolf is the Grandmother's friend and they had been to visit Pam's family, including the cat, to bring them love.

They wanted to encourage Pam and her family in their spiritual development and ascension. They were also assuring them that their loved ones were okay in the spirit world.

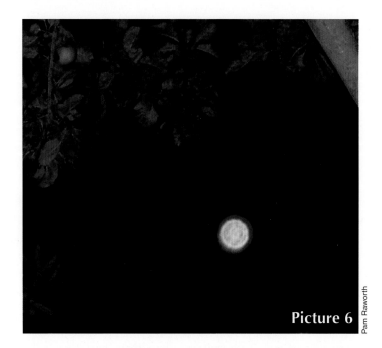

Pam Raworth

Picture 6

Lone Wolf is one of the guides of Kathy's husband, Paul. Paul told me that, as a child he was scared of wolves, and being psychic he kept seeing them round him. As he grew older he realised they were there because they were with Lone Wolf. He added that Lone Wolf was a Kiowa chief in a Native American life and was a father figure to him, yet at the same time he was full of fun and mischief. Paul said, 'When he is around you have the feeling that everything is alright'.

Lone Wolf

When you look at Orb (6) you receive a feeling that everything is alright.

***

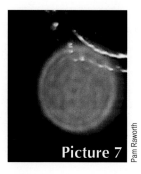

Picture 7

Pam also took many wonderful Orb pictures at my annual Angel Awareness Day seminar in 2007. One of them, picture (7) contained angels of Archangels Zadkiel, Gabriel< Metatron and Michael as well as her spirit guide. Her guide was holding her consciousness at the right level so that she could take the Orb photographs. I find it helpful to remember that I can ask my guide to hold my frequency steady at the right level for what I am intending to accomplish for the highest good – and you may find this useful too.

Angels of Archangels Zadkiel, Gabriel, Metatron and Michael and a spirit guide

When you look at picture (7) you receive a knowing that you are guided.

Chapter Five

The Angelic Kingdom

Elemental kingdom

The lowest of the angelic kingdom are the elementals. Amongst them are fairies, gnomes, goblins, elves, fauns, salamanders, undines, mermaids, kyhils, esaks and dragons.

Angels

Angels are messengers from God and amongst them are guardian angels, who look after you and keep your personal records for you. At a higher frequency, below the archangels are many levels of angels, from angels of protection or peace to angels of love.

Archangels

Archangels serve in a cosmic capacity and are responsible for the angels below them. They or their angels sometimes merge together to shine great light on you, as you will see from the orbs in this book.

Unicorns

Unicorns are seventh dimensional creatures, ascended horses who are fully of the angelic hierarchy. They have the same frequency as archangels and are returning now for the first time since the fall of Atlantis to shine wonder and enlightenment on us. They offer healing through their horns of light and are looking for those who have a vision to help others beside themselves. Then they will work with you to give you the strength and courage, dignity and purity to fulfil your purpose.

Your unicorn helps you activate the desires of your soul and expand your levels of enlightenment to reach the ascension pathway.

In picture (8) a unicorn is surrounding the moon, radiating enlightenment to all who are open to it.

Picture 8

Einav Adir

A unicorn

When you look at Orb (8) you will receive healing and a desire to bring oneness to the world.

***

Principalities

Faster frequency than the archangels are the principalities, who oversee huge organisations like hospitals, big corporations and government offices. They look after towns and cities, schools, sacred sites, countries and huge events or projects.

In picture (9) you can see an Orb with three heads. The lower part of the Orb is a power, the frequency above principalities.

He is Wywyvsil, who is activating or powering the three principalities for there is a crisis in the area. They in turn are giving instructions to one of Archangel Gabriel's angels, the bright Orb above them. All the Orbs are bringing spirits and some are angels of love bringing spirits of animals who loved this place. There are also tiny dots which are fairies.

Picture 9

Mandy Whalley

Wywyvsil is bringing forward karma that has been blocking your life, in a way that you can deal with it. He is also clearing collective karma. These Orbs will lift your level of enlightenment and bring a higher perspective on life and the world.

A power, principalities and Archangel Gabriel's angel bringing spirits

When you look at picture (9) you receive enlightenment about just how much help is available to humanity.

***

Powers

The powers include the Lords of Karma, who preside over the Akashic Records, and Angels of Death and Birth. There is more information about the Lords of Karma in Chapter 7.

Virtues

Virtues are sending huge beams of light to Earth to facilitate the changes in consciousness, which are taking place now.

Dominions

Dominions oversee the angelic hierarchy below them, offer mercy to humanity and are helping us ascend.

Thrones

Thrones receive illumination directly from Source and then they transform the divine wisdom into frequencies that humanity can accept. They look after the planets, for example, Lady Gaia is the throne in charge of Earth.

Cherubim

Cherubim are angels of wisdom and are the guardians of the stars and the heavens.

Cherubs

Cherubs work with the cherubim, in the same way as angels work with arch-angels.

The cherubs help with the stars and work with those who are universal angel ambassadors. The frequency of the cherubs is not as high as the thrones but higher than the principalities. When the people who lived during the Renaissance saw cherubs they were seeing a tiny energy fragment of cherubim. When unicorns are at a distance we see a small very bright light. When they are close the light is larger, softer and diffused. The energy of the cherubs works in the same way. When they appear to be very bright and clear they are a long way away.

Why were cherubs depicted as babies, and therefore seen by mystics in that way?

Mainly because when people connected with them they felt light, joy and pure innocence. During the time of the Renaissance many more angels came to Earth, just as they are doing now. However in those times many people suffered from fevers and these opened the veil between the worlds, so that they could see the cherubs. But the cherubim resonated on too high a frequency and could not be seen. So illness often opens a window of opportunity.

Who connects with cherubs?

Those who feel vulnerable identify with them, while those who love the stars and expanded universes have an automatic connection.

How can we connect with cherubim?

You need a high level of purification and the unicorns or Archangel Gabriel can help you with this. You can connect with them by meditating on an Orb of a cherubim or the Mary Orb on the back cover, by looking at the stars or by going to the Pyramids or looking at a picture of them.

What is the benefit of linking to the cherubim

Most importantly they help people connect to their planet of origin. They also assist you to link to the fourth planet Neptune, which was known as the hidden planet. The other three stars important for the ascension of Earth are Orion, Sirius and the Pleiades. When you have made your connection with all four this will heal Mother Earth and help her ascend. You will also have a new understanding of the awesomeness of Creation.

Seraphim

The seraphim, whose essence is pure love, are the highest of the spiritual hierarchy of angels. They surround the Godhead and create the harmonics, which hold the vibration of Creation, then direct the energy from Source.

They do not normally interact with humans except to move big projects forward for the ascension of the planet. We have been very privileged in writing the Orbs books that various Seraphim have communicated through us several times. Seraphina, whose great crystal ball is to the right beyond your Stellar Gateway chakra as you look up told us that they had done so because spreading the light of the Orbs is considered most important.

Seraphina, a feminine energy, is helping to draw humanity to ascension.

Seraphisa, a feminine energy, is helping to relax and de-stress humanity so that we can connect with our hearts. This will help people find compassion. Source specifically directed her to do this work.

Seraphiel, a masculine energy, works to keep the universe in order. Because the current low consciousness on Earth is holding back the divine plan he is focussing his attention on us. He is especially trying to influence those who are influential and could accelerate change. It is Seraphiel in pictures (10) and (48).

Orb (10) contains Seraphiel, one of the mighty Seraphim. He came to the location in this picture to create a higher energy here, as this particular place is often visited by those who live solely in a material world. When such people sit or shelter under the tree, the energy switches them on and awakens them spiritually.

Paul the Venetian has arrived with Seraphiel to bring such individuals freedom

Picture 10

Tammie Stair

from their lower consciousness and to expand the limited world they inhabit. Most people on Earth have some mental limitations and this Orb can bring a higher and broader perspective.

The Seraphim Seraphiel, an angel of Archangel Uriel, with Paul the Venetian

When you look at Orb (10) you receive freedom to move into an expanded life.

Chapter Six

Archangels and Ascension

Archangels

Archangels assist our ascension more than we can have any concept of. While your guardian angel holds the vision for you of your highest spiritual potential, the archangels light up this possibility and open higher doors.

In the next section we offer wonderful new information about the archangels who are in charge of the development of the twelve chakras. We also introduce you to their twin flames or archaea who hold the divine feminine balance for them. In *Ascension through Orbs* we show you Orb pictures of many of these archangels, which will help you to awaken, open and activate the twelve chakras, including the transpersonal ones, to accelerate your ascension.

Archangel rays

Each archangel works on one ray, so they only beam down that particular colour and energy. This is why we show so many Orbs in which two or more archangels have merged their light, enabling them to radiate different qualities. I describe picture (22) in chapter 15, in which Archangel Michael himself is radiating his light into two of Archangel Gabriel and Uriel's angels, so that they have the strength and protection to counteract human fear, while they accomplish a particular piece of work. Without the Michael light, they could not do this.

Archangel Gem rays

The archangels have the power to reach deep into the Earth and activate certain rocks with their light. These then become gems or crystals.

When people wear them, look at them or hold them, they can access the qualities of the archangel. This is why powerful people used to wear precious stones.

Looking at archangel Orbs offers the same energy to the masses and meditating with crystals, gems and Orbs together enhances the effect of both.

Gabriel	Diamond	Clarity, purification, joy, permanence
Michael	Sapphire	Protection, strength, courage
Raphael	Emerald	Healing, abundance, mental clarity and power
Uriel	Ruby	Confidence, self worth, love
Chamuel	Rose quartz	Love, compassion, empathy
Metatron	Gold	Wisdom, commitment, discipline
Sandalphon	Silver	Psychic awareness and spirituality
Jophiel	Citrine	Prosperity, good fortune
Zadkiel	Amethyst	Higher connections, transmutation

Archangel promotions and new archangels

The Angels of Mercy who were at the top of the hierarchy of angels, have now in turn reached the frequency level of archangels.

Archaons

The big seven, those archangels who are best known and loved for their unfailing service to humanity; Archangels Michael, Uriel, Gabriel, Raphael, Chamuel, Jophiel and Zadkiel have raised their frequency to such a level that they have now become Archaons, which is a level slightly lower than the principalities, those who are in charge of major projects for Earth.

Archangels Metatron and Sandalphon are also Archaons. In addition Archangels Purlimiek, Gersisa, Butyalil and Fhelyai (pronounced Felyay), who are less well known but who have been working for the betterment of nature, animals and the planet have also risen to this rank. There are Orbs of Archangels Purlimiek, Gersisa and Butyalil later in this book. You can see Archangel Fhelyai in picture (46).

Archangels collect you when you ascend

When you ascend as you pass over, many archangels and masters come to collect you – and there is rejoicing in the heavens.

Archangels accompany masters

When the masters journey through the inner planes, they are accompanied by archangels. Each of these archangels brings their special energy to the task in hand, as they enfold the master. You will see many Orbs in this book as they travel with particular archangels for protection or to help them radiate love, peace, healing or some important quality.

Travelling in the Christ light

Even the greatest of the masters cannot travel without an angel, unless they are within the Christ light, which offers its own protection. We learnt this in the very early days of our study of Orbs when we were looking at a picture which had been sent to us of a dark sky at night. In it we could see the face of a master. My guide, Kumeka, kept saying to us, 'What is different about this one?' At last we realised what it was: there was no angel Orb round him! And then we saw that he was within a golden mist and understood that he was travelling in the greatest of all protective energies, the Christ light.

Does an angel accompany a stuck soul?

Spirits of those who have not passed and are stuck or lost are always accompanied by an elemental called a wuryl. They are rarely conscious of this but no one is ever alone.

Spirits travelling

Spirits of those who have passed or those who are travelling out of body are always accompanied by their guardian angel and sometimes also with an archangel if their frequency is high enough.

Archangel Gabriel collecting spirits

I took photograph (11) in my garden, when I came home one evening. Archangels Gabriel, Mallory and Uriel are collecting spirits who were lost and are taking them in joyously. (The archangels are filled with delight and so are the spirits). Lady Gaia, often known as Mother Earth, is merged with the archangels and Seraphiel the Seraphim, is holding the energy. It is all contained within the Source light.

There are nearly always Archangel Gabriel's angels in my garden and I often wondered why. I was also aware that sometimes the area is absolutely full of souls waiting to pass. We were told that my work in this house creates an energy which enables souls to progress, so they are drawn to it.

This Orb offers a message for all who are raising awareness of the light. You too will attract spirits who need help to pass. They need your help and you need protection.

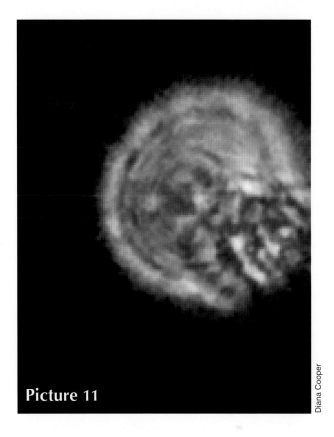

Picture 11

Diana Cooper

Archangels Gabriel, Mallory and Uriel collecting spirits

When you look at picture (11) you receive a reminder that there are many stuck or lost souls who will be drawn to your light. Remember them and protect yourself.

***

How to help souls who come to you

It is very simple. Put on your protection, and I would suggest Michael's blue cloak and the Christ light. Then sit quietly and call on Mother Mary to come to collect this person. Sense, intuit or watch what is happening for the spirit and gently encourage it to turn to the light. When it finally sees where to go, it usually shoots happily off and you may have a sense of loved ones coming to meet it. Remember to thank Mother Mary and the angels who accompany her.

Chapter Seven

The Powers and Lords of Karma

The lowest of the angelic hierarchy are the Guardian Angels, then the many kinds of angels. Above them are the wondrous archangels and, at yet a higher frequency, are the principalities, those of the angel realms who look after cities, international organisations, governments and large projects. The next rank of angels is the powers and amongst these awesome beings are the Lords of Karma and the angels of birth and death.

The Lords of Karma take decisions about personal, town, country and world karma. Until recently there have been seven Lords of Karma, each presiding over one of the seven rays on Earth. Now that the twelve rays have been established there are twelve Lords of Karma. These are distinct from the Masters or Chohans of the rays, though in some instances one master has overlapping responsibilities.

The Lords of Karma are:

Ray 1	The Great Divine Director	The Great Divine Director has never incarnated and is not of this universe or any other. He is very close to God and thinks things through for the divine plan.
Ray 2	The Goddess of Liberty	The Goddess of Liberty was a High Priestess in the Temple of Liberty in Atlantis. She works a little with individuals to help them to be mentally and emotionally free. Mostly however she holds the Flame of Freedom with Paul the Venetian to enable humanity to walk the ascension path. It is time for people to be free to experience Earth as we were intended to. Her task is to bring back the energy of Golden Atlantis.
Ray 3	Lady Nada	Lady Nada is the Lord of Karma for the third ray and in addition the master of the seventh ray.

Ray 4	Pallas Athena	The Goddess of Truth
Ray 5	Elohim Vista	The Elohim are the Creator Angels.
Ray 6	Quan Yin	The Goddess of Mercy who had a 2000 year incarnation in China. She spreads the divine feminine.
Ray 7	Lady Portia	The Goddess of Justice and spokesperson for the Karmic Board.
Ray 8	Jesus	Jesus is now the Lord of Karma for this ray. He was co-working with Lord Meitreya, Overlord for the Planet and Lord Kuthumi, World Teacher but he has now moved on and has a new role as Bringer of Cosmic Love. One aspect of Jesus is currently incarnated on Earth as a healer called Paul who works with the Christ Consciousness.
Ray 9	Josiah	Josiah comes from Sirius. He was in incarnated in Pompeii when it was destroyed by a volcano and, when he passed, his spirit made itself into a bridge to help others, some of whom ascended. He worked with Archangel Uriel, remaining calm and centred, and knew exactly what to do. He still helps with the consequences of volcanoes and earthquakes.
Ray 10	Abraham	An aspect of El Morya, master of the first ray.
Ray 11	Peter the Great	Peter the Great had many incarnations and ascended after a lifetime in Russia. He was very in tune with nature and the animal kingdom, and now helps movements which take care of the environment, reforestation, clearing rivers and other similar themes. When people who have polluted the planet pass over, he works with them to help them understand the impact of what they have done. He co-ordinates with Archangel Purlimiek, the angel of nature, and the elemental masters. His task is to assist with cleansing, right back to the devastating atom bombs which were set off in one of the early experiments of Atlantis.

Ray 12	Catherine of Sienna	St Catherine is helping to stimulate the spiritual light within humanity. In previous incarnations she was Joan of Arc and Helena Blavatsky, who brought Theosophy to the world.

Picture 12

Patti McCullough

**Archangel Christiel with the Master Josiah,
Lord of Karma for the 9th ray**

When you look at Orb (12) you receive a sense of the fairness of the universe.

✳✳✳

Picture 13

Patti McCullough

Archangel Mariel, Peter the Great, Lord of Karma for the 11th ray

When you look at Orb (13) you receive a deep connection with nature.

***

The Angels of Birth and Death

When you are born an angel of birth conducts your spirit to your birth mother and accompanies you during the entry. Your guardian angel is also present.

No one dies alone. An angel of death is with you as is your guardian angel. Other angels may come to collect you and, naturally, the spirits of your loved ones are waiting for you.

Wywyvsil – His role as an angel of birth

Wywyvsil is a Lord of Karma and in charge of the Angels of Birth. Source and Wywyvsil decide who incarnates, for a place on this planet is highly prized. There are souls throughout the universes who long for a chance to take a body here because the opportunities for spiritual growth are monumental. There is no other plane of existence which offers sexuality, sensations, emotions and a physical body; nor does anywhere else provide a feedback mechanism like a body. Every cell of your body blocks or flows, dims or lights, is unhealthy or healthy according to the messages you send with your thoughts and emotions.

Having agreed with Source who is to incarnate on Earth, it is Wywyvsil's mighty task to supervise where and to whom they will be born. For this there is consultation with the archangel and guides, as well as with the higher selves of their proposed parents and siblings.

Challenges and opportunities have to be decided, as does the purpose and lessons for that lifetime. Karma has to be weighed and so do the longings of the soul. The place and time of birth is also important. What are the atmospherics like in that location? Is this a familiar area to the soul or completely unknown, and what effect will this have? What are the astrological impacts of the time choices? How do all the life plans of billions of humans fit together?

Supervising your life

Before you incarnate you are allocated to an archangel, who oversees your progress. Then when you have been born, Wywyvsil works with your archangel. At first you also have a spirit guide who works with you and then you progress to a teaching guide, finally an ascended master. If your ascension is borderline this great power helps you become a fully ascended master.

Teaching in the inner planes

In the inner places Wywyvsil has set up a number of schools to teach healing, enlightenment and transformation to those who have sufficient light. If you qualify you may ask that your spirit can attend in your sleep.

He has created a school where Earth spirits and those of other planets meet and get to know and understand each other.

He also organises a school for those from Sirius, the Pleiades and Orion, who are connected with healing through the Egyptian connection.

The Atlantean Pool of Energy

Wywyvsil was one of those who created a pool of energy for healing, transformation and enlightenment, including the original pure Reiki, for all to access as they did in Atlantis. From it he is sending light directly to Earth. All the High Priests and Priestesses of Atlantis, except Voosloo, are keys to access the energy. And all Orbs of the angelic hierarchy are also keys.

Working with the seraphim

Wywyvsil is working with the seraphim to help creation.

Connection with Kathy Crosswell

Wywyvsil is of the angelic hierarchy, who has worked with Kathy Crosswell in 101 previous lives on various planets and universes. He is currently guiding her and has been connecting with both of us as we wrote this series of Orbs books.

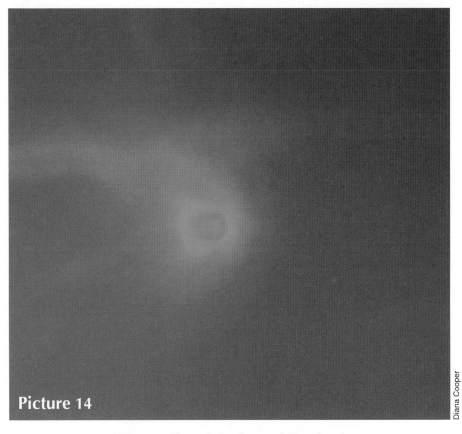

Picture 14

Diana Cooper

Wywyvsil and Archangel Raphael

When I took the picture of Orb (14) I was waiting for a friend to arrive, as we were going for a walk together. I idly snapped away, sometimes at the sun, at other times at the trees. Every photo that I took towards the sun had this green and yellow Orb in it. I was so amazed that I thought it must be a trick of the light and decided to delete them but something stopped me. When Kathy and I talked to Kumeka he told us that it was Archangel Raphael with

Wywyvsil. They had a special message for me and everyone else who is drawn to this Orb.

Archangel Raphael is bringing healing and Wywyvsil is helping to clear karma. He is bringing things up so that they hit you in the face and you have to deal with it. This is in order to accelerate your process. You may also feel the urgency of healing the planet.

A few weeks later I was again leaning on my car waiting for a friend when I took some pictures towards the sun. As I did so I thought about the time that Archangels Raphael and Wywyvsil had appeared. To my shock this Orb was once again in those pictures. Once more I decided that it was a trick of the light and I must check both photograph sessions.

This time Archangel Raphael came in and confirmed that the Orbs were Wywyvsil and himself. He said that I had called them in with my thought and added that I was going to have a very challenging and important week, so they were giving me healing. (This resonated for it had already started!)

When you look at Orb (14) you will receive an acceleration of your ascension.

Section Two

The 12 Chakras and Archangels

Chapter Eight

The Chakras

What is a chakra?

Chakra literally means wheel or circle in Sanskrit because, when they are active, they are seen as round revolving balls of light. They are spiritual energy centres which take in divine light, absorb it and radiate it out into the aura. They also filter it down to the chakras below them. They act as valves. If you imagine each one as a water lily or daisy, the petals open when the sun shines down onto them and then close when the light dims.

Light contains spiritual knowledge so while the petals are open the flower is receiving cosmic information, which they integrate when they close. If it is a tightly closed bud nothing can enter and there is no spiritual growth. This affects the other flowers on the stalk. In humans your spine is the conduit through which energy flows, connecting the chakras. If one is not working, there will be a blockage below it, which may eventually result in ill health.

A chakra can move in any direction, which means it can seek information or illumination as appropriate. Your base chakra for example will be directed at the ground if it is looking for somewhere for you to put down your roots. If you are seeking a job it might be wide open with its antennae searching everywhere. When you have evolved to a life based on spirituality, your chakras will seek high frequency sustenance for you.

Third dimensional chakras

Third dimensional people, those who believe that their power, safety and happiness lie in possessions are acting from fear and illusion. They have seven chakras which vibrate at a low frequency. Of course, it is an enormous challenge to live in a material world, surrounded by people who measure success by the size of their bank account, their security by alarms and walls and who mistake attachment for love. Nevertheless we have all signed on to be on Earth now with its awesome opportunity for spiritual growth. Happily for most of us you do not have to be perfect to start opening up your twelve chakras. Even the great ascended masters still have some ego. You can make the transformation now.

Fourth dimensional chakras

As people wake up spiritually and start to evolve, their frequency rises and their chakras become fourth dimensional. The colours start to refine and they spin more quickly. Most importantly their heart centres start to open, so that they seek reconciliation and peace. They want to heal their family history. They also love themselves more, so they will not tolerate being treated with a lack of respect. On a global level, openheartedness will result in more peace movements and fairer treatment of women for example

The other consequence of a rise in consciousness is that people become more open minded and aware that religions are all valid paths to God. Then they become accepting of the beliefs of others. They also start to accept the principle of past lives and even remember their own.

Fifth dimensional chakras

When you raise your frequency to a fifth dimensional level you feel empathy for the whole of humanity and promote equality, fairness and oneness. You treat others as you would like to be treated. You accept that you have created your life and that as a master you have the power to change it. (As a human being you are allowed a few blips!) Then the colours of your chakras become more subtle and clear and you are ready to wake up the five chakras that have been dormant. You are on your way to re-establishing your full twelve chakras.

Chapter Nine

The 12 Chakras & Archangels

In the time of Golden Atlantis when the people vibrated at a fifth dimensional frequency and were fully enlightened they had twelve fully operational chakras. This enabled them to connect with Source and live as ascended masters. Because of this they literally glowed with light and had access to awesome spiritual and psychic gifts.

Currently all these gifts and powers are latent within us, waiting for the re-awakening of the five chakras which closed down as Atlantis devolved.

Now for the first time since the fall, we all have the opportunity to raise our frequency again, open the twelve chakras and access our full divine potential. The Orbs can help you do this.

The fifth dimensional chakras are obviously a much higher frequency than the third dimensional ones that most people are accustomed to. The colours, therefore, are lighter and faster and may feel less familiar to you.

The twelve chakras and the archangels who oversee them

The Earth Star

Archangel Sandalphon, the twin flame of Archangel Metatron of the Stellar Gateway, works with this chakra. The universal angel Roquiel and his twin flame Joules, takes the Earth Star understandings to a deeper connection with Lady Gaia. Archangel Joules works deep in the oceans and one of his tasks is to govern the alignment of the tectonic places.

The Earth Star chakra is black and white.

The base, sacral and navel chakras

Archangel Gabriel and his twin flame Hope are in charge and have developed what used to be one chakra in humans until it has differentiated into these three chakras. At the fifth dimension the base chakra is platinum, the sacral is tender pink and the navel is bright orange.

The solar plexus chakra

Archangel Uriel and his twin flame Aurora absorb negativity, strengthen your confidence and bring back your wisdom. At the fifth dimensional frequency the solar plexus chakra is deep gold with rainbow lights.

The heart chakra

Archangels Chamuel and Charity open your heart to its deepest levels. This is a central junction and all archangels link into the heart centre.

At the fifth dimensional frequency the heart chakra is white.

The throat chakra

Archangels Michael and Faith help you strengthen this chakra of mastery, strength and truth. At the fifth dimensional frequency the throat chakra is royal blue.

The third eye

This chakra is in the charge of Archangel Raphael and his twin flame Mary. When the veils are removed at the fifth dimension this chakra is a crystal ball.

The crown chakra

Archangel Jophiel and his twin flame Christine hold this chakra, which is at the top of the head. Christine brings in the Christ light. The thousand petalled lotus is crystal clear at the fifth dimension.

The causal chakra

Archangel Christiel and his twin flame Mallory, the Keeper of Ancient Wisdom, help to anchor this chakra, which is above the crown chakra, to the back of the head. It requires feminine energy to do this task. This chakra is white.

The soul star chakra

You are prepared by Archangels Zadkiel and Amethyst to enter this chakra. When you are ready Archangels Mariel and Lavender introduce you to a deeper understanding. We discuss them and the initiation journey into this centre in Chapter 19. This chakra is magenta.

The Stellar Gateway

Archangel Metatron looks after this, the highest chakra. There is a stage between the Stellar Gateway and Source. The Seraphim Seraphina is in charge of this and she works at a higher frequency than Archangel Metatron. This chakra is deepest gold to orange.

An ascension portal

Patti McCullough sent us so many glorious Orbs, mostly taken near a hammock where her mother sat during her last visit. We asked why so many wonderful Orbs appeared here and were told that Patti's mother ascended when she passed, for she had great qualities of gentleness. She left her energy in this place and created an ascension portal. However, it is Patti's consciousness which has drawn in the spectacular Orbs including the rainbow Orb (15) and (16)), which contains Archangels Uriel, Michael, Metatron, Gabriel and Raphael and is bringing several masters as well as spirits. The four great beings travelling in this Orb are Serapis Bey, Paul the Venetian and Lord Meitreya. Mother Mary herself is bringing in the divine feminine.

The spirits are other deceased relatives who have come here to radiate their light. They are putting their energy into the earth and it is going right down to the Hollow Earth. This means that a shaft of light is connected from Source, through this place into the core of the planet to accelerate everyone's ascension. Anyone who physically visits this location will pick up this energy.

Picture 15

Orb of Archangels Uriel, Michael, Metatron, Gabriel and Raphael with Serapis Bey, Paul the Venetian, Lord Meitreya, Mother Mary and spirits

When you look at Orbs (15) and (16) you receive a boost on your ascension pathway.

The colours of this Orb are in layers because each Archangel remains individual, rather than merging their energies. Archangel Uriel is bringing peace, Archangel Michael holds courage, Archangel Metatron is issuing an invitation to ascension, Archangel Gabriel radiates clarity and Archangel Raphael sends healing.

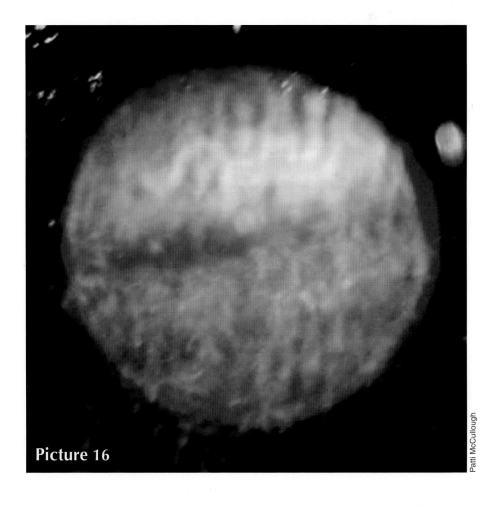

Picture 16

Patti McCullough

Chapter Ten

Preparation for the 12 Chakras

The unicorns, Angels of Atlantis, ascended masters and many wise ones are visiting Earth at this important time, helping us to attune to fifth dimensional frequencies: those of love, grace and oneness. They are waiting to assist us to transcend our lower limitations and move into the spiritual dimensions. Most important are the quality of our intention and our willingness to practise a spiritual discipline.

There are many valid spiritual disciplines. I have tried chanting mantras, prayer, journal writing, meditation, yoga, tai chi, peace breathing amongst others but I confess I am a bit of a grasshopper and soon move on to something else. In fact, bearing in mind one of my favourite stories about Gandhi I was about to scrub this paragraph, when I was reminded that my spiritual discipline is my writing and this I have unfailingly practised.

Here is the story about Gandhi that I often tell. A woman walked for half a day through the baking heat to bring her overweight son to the Mahatma. When they reached the front of the queue she said to him, "Please tell my son to stop eating sugar." Gandhi is said to have asked them to return the following week. So, one week later, she once more traipsed through the heat to see the wise guru with her fat son in tow. This time when she asked Gandhi to tell her boy to stop eating sugar, he spoke to the boy, 'Do as your mother says and stop eating sugar'. "But why didn't you say that last week," the woman protested angrily, "We've walked for hours to see you." Gandhi replied, "First I had to give it up myself."

Integrity is vital in order to open the 12 chakras.

It is helpful to have a daily practice, even if it is only as simple as lighting a candle when you wake up and dedicating it to your higher purpose that day.

Here are some simple daily practices.

* A daily walk dedicated to your unicorn or angel connection.
* Sending out healing to specific people or the world.

* Lighting candles, dedicating them to helping those in need.
* Hug a tree and send it love and gratitude.
* Walk round your garden and appreciate the flowers and grass.
* Chant the Aum (om) or other mantra for five minutes.

Chapter Eleven

The Earth Star Chakra

About 12″ (30cms) below your feet lies the Earth Star, which contains your life purpose and holds your invitation from Lady Gaia to be on Earth.

When your Earth Star is awake and open you are absolutely clear about your life purpose.

This black chakra is the link between your spiritual self and your earthly self. It is only when this chakra is totally awake that the Stellar Gateway can fully accept the light of Source and pass it down through your chakras into every cell of your body and into Lady Gaia herself. Then you can fully heal yourself and do your part to renew our planet.

It is the light of the Stellar Gateway, soul star and causal chakras that stimulates this earthly chakra to open, so it all happens simultaneously. This means that we have to activate the Earth Star at the same time as the three upper chakras.

The preparation of the Earth Star is as vital for ascension as is the solid construction of the foundations of a tower block for its safety.

How to awaken and open your Earth Star Chakra

There are 33 petals or chambers in this chakra and when each of these is open and awake, your Earth Star Chakra is fully operational.

This is what you must do to activate each of the chambers.

Acknowledge and accept your connection to Earth.

1. Actively honour Earth.
2. Appreciate and revel in the beauty of it.
3. Walk on Earth with awareness, knowing it is a two way connection.
4. Actively give to Earth through your twelve chakras.
5. Actively receive from the Earth.
6. Honour the produce of the Earth.

7. Dig in the soil.
8. Touch and honour the trees.
9. Plant trees.
10. Walk barefoot in the grass.
11. Acknowledge and honour the flowers.
12. Honour the waters of the Earth.
13. Respect the air (the prana).
14. Honour the transmuting qualities of fire.
15. Sense the nurturing qualities of the earth.
16. Honour the animals on Earth.
17. Honour the reptiles.
18. Honour the birds.
19. Honour the greenery, the leaves and grass, and the process of photosynthesis.
20. Honour the rocks and stones as keepers of ancient history.
21. Be grateful for the crystals and send healing to the Earth where they have been dug out.
22. Accept the relevance of the stars in their connection with Earth.
23. Accept the lessons of the dolphins.
24. Honour all other marine life.
25. Honour all humans.
26. Accept oneness – that everything is part of God.
27. Honour the masculine power and light of the sun.
28. Honour the feminine qualities of the moon.
29. Honour the Egyptian, Mayan and all other pyramids.
30. Honour the mountains.
31. Honour the forests.
32. Honour the spiritual world.
33. Accept the other dimensions.

Preparing for the opening of your Earth Star

In Orb (17) Archangels Michael and Uriel have come together with a unicorn and the Master El Morya in order to help you prepare for the awakening of your Earth Star.

Archangel Michael is bringing courage. Archangel Uriel offers the energy to cope with challenges, for everyone on the ascension pathway meets tests and challenges.

The unicorn is holding the ascension flame and making sure that you stay on your ascension pathway in a difficult time.

This Orb is specifically for people who have had a loss, whether it is bereavement or the loss of a job or way of life. It also calls in loved ones to help. As you work with this Orb it does not just help you with your loss but also brings you trust and optimism and accelerates your ascension.

Picture 17

Eugene Mc Gill

Archangels Michael, Uriel, a Unicorn and El Morya

When you look at picture (17) you will receive courage, healing and support on your ascension pathway.

***

Archangel Sandalphon

Archangel Sandalphon helps you to take your roots firmly down to the deeper levels, where you can make your unique connection with Lady Gaia, the highly evolved being of the angelic realms, a throne, who looks after Earth.

Archangel Sandalphon is known as 'He who wears sandals before God,' because he is the angel who takes prayers to Him. He is also called the tall angel because he bridges Earth and heaven. We were sent a picture of the angel of a church who had gathered all the prayers which had been offered there and Kumeka my guide told me the angel was waiting to give them to Sandalphon to take to Source.

Prayer is a solidly grounding spiritual practice

Archangel Sandalphon's twin flame is Archangel Metatron, who works with the Stellar Gateway, the access to Source. The Stellar Gateway cannot flourish without the Earth Star, or vice versa. You have to provide good soil for the roots of a plant *and* place it where it receives sunshine.

In the extraordinary Orb (18) taken by Tammie Stair, four great archangels have merged their energy and it affects you unconsciously when you look at it. Archangel Sandalphon has come to help you prepare your Earth Star to be awakened and, if it is already awake, he is anchoring you more deeply to your spiritual path.

Archangel Gabriel is purifying your consciousness so that you will be ready to accept your Earth Star chakra.

Archangel Christiel is helping you to still your mind so that you can awaken your transcendent chakras and bring energy through from Source.

Archangel Mallory is holding your energy so that you are in peace and your intentions are positive.

The spirits within this Orb have already accomplished the above. They have all passed and are in the process of ascending. By holding this consciousness they are making it easier for you to do so too. Celebrating the opening of the Earth Star Chakra is very important.

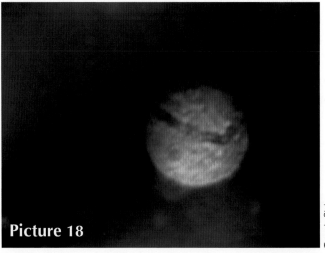

Picture 18

Tammie Stair

Archangels Sandalphon, Gabriel, Christiel and Mallory with spirits

When you look at Orb (18) you celebrate the awakening of your Earth Star chakra, which is the rite of passage to the next step of your ascension journey.

***

Archangel Roquiel

It is Archangel Roquiel, with his twin flame Archangel Joules, who helps the Stellar Gateway and the Earth Star to open simultaneously. He takes energy from the Earth star to Lady Gaia. Humans are bridges to Source, so Archangel Roquiel holds all the energy that comes down through them, then sends it out in a form that Gaia can use. He also directs it to the right people, to the portals, the leylines and especially to the pyramids. He is one of the universal angels of the seraphim rank.

In addition he sends this energy to the four starts and planets connected with Earth's ascension, Orion, Sirius, Pleiades and the hidden planet, Neptune. When Neptune is re-connected Earth will ascend. Archangel Joules works with the deepest oceans.

Banita Kern sent us an extraordinary Orb (19) of Archangel Roquiel with Archangel Sandalphon. Archangel Roquiel is the white aspect of the Orb while Archangel Sandalphon is the grey-black Orb. Together the black and white represent the masculine and feminine, the yang and yin.

The Orb is radiating energy to the area, helping people to connect to their Earth Star chakra and to the Great Pyramid. These two angelic beings travel together all over the world to send out this message to all who are ready. Because this Orb helps you to connect deep into the earth and up to the heavens, it assists you to awaken your kundalini. It also makes you into a pure channel from Source to the centre of Earth.

Archangels Roquiel and Sandalphon

When you look at Orb (19) you receive a connection deep into the earth and up to the heavens to assist your ascension.

Picture 19

Banita Kern

Chapter Twelve

The Base, Sacral and Navel Chakras

These three chakras are in the charge of Archangel Gabriel and his twin flame, Archangel Hope.

In primitive humans these were combined as one chakra. Archangel Gabriel helped our species to separate the survival energies from the sexual ones, so the chakra differentiated into two chakras, one red and the other orange. This is where most of humanity, those at a third dimensional level, still remain but this is changing rapidly.

In Golden Atlantis, with fifth dimensional frequencies flowing through the people, these became three separate chakras; base, sacral or sexual and navel.

The base chakra

When this chakra vibrates at a fifth dimensional level you step onto the ascension pathway. It becomes platinum, indicating total trust in the Universe to provide for your safety and security. It reflects the development of good spiritual practices and as it opens Archangel Gabriel helps you to connect with the sacred wisdom of the dolphins.

This chakra has two petals or chambers, each of which is dedicated to living in a grounded way on the planet. The journey starts at the third dimension with fear based survival and the instinctive reaction to challenges by fight or flight. At this level the chakra is constantly open, desperately seeking security. It spins too fast, creating anxiety, or it may spin too slowly resulting in depression. The story of this chakra is the journey to trust. Archangel Hope is constantly beaming light here to sustain you.

In order to experience completely the benefits of your incarnation you must be grounded, which involves having your feet chakra open. These send down psychic roots into the ground to enable you to drink in Earth energies, which will support and sustain you on a daily basis. This prana will be drawn up your chakra system to merge with the spiritual light coming down. You can then pass the higher frequencies down through your feet chakra into the earth. When this process works properly this enables you to be in touch with reality at all times.

For ascension the whole process must go much deeper and higher. When you ascend to higher energies you become a conductor which links heaven and Earth, so you must be able to anchor yourself thoroughly, access deeper Earth energies and connect with the leylines before the Source light can pass through you.

There is an axiom that you cannot go higher than you can dig deep, and it is true. The simple analogy is this. If you are putting up a small shed it only needs a shallow base. However, to establish a tall edifice you must ensure it has deep, strong foundations for many lives may depend on the safe grounding of this building. Your spiritual structure has exactly the same needs for, as above, so it is below.

How to anchor your base chakra

This chakra embodies the principle of being on the planet but not of it. This means enjoying all the experiences that incarnation offers, yet remaining connected to your spiritual knowing.

Family, friends, your work, your home and hobbies are your support structure. It is worth reviewing your relationships, how satisfying you find your job or hobbies and whether your home is somewhere you enjoy living. If you are not getting what you need from these, consider what changes you can make.

Good eating habits and an exercise regime all contribute to your foundations on Earth, so make healthy, vitalising decisions now. It is these seemingly earthly matters that help to consolidate your base chakra.

Spiritual practices ground you deeply and I discuss these later.

Anything that involves touching the earth, such as walking, especially in bare feet, helps to anchor and purify your base centre. It does not have the same effect if you are on tarmac or concrete as you cannot draw in energy through these mediums.

I had a headache one day and felt very tired, so I went down to the beach and walked along the promenade. I soon realised that I wasn't feeling any better because I was on concrete, so I moved down the sand to the water's edge. Within minutes my headache had vanished and so had my fatigue.

Petals or chambers of the base chakra

This chakra has two petals of balance, so these represent the masculine and feminine, independence and dependence, yang and yin. It is in bringing these to balance that you align this chakra with ascension.

Sacral chakra

At its highest expression the sacral or sexual chakra becomes a pale, soft pink, enabling your expression of sexuality to become tender, loving, honouring and respectful. At this level sexuality becomes transcendent.

There are sixteen chambers or petals in this chakra, which represent the journey to ascension for this centre

Where the focus is on self

If you are not aligned to the heart your focus will be on steps 1-5, where you are at the level of the manipulative, needy, greedy inner child. You feel unfulfilled and are too scared of emotional attachment to be fulfilled. You can be cruel and paedophiles are stuck here.

1. Sexuality for control. Many people in the third dimensional reality use their sexuality to manipulate or get what they need for themselves, for example they offer comfort in order to receive something in exchange. It is when someone's sexual chakra is stuck at this level that they are interested in child porn or become stalkers.
2. A feeling of powerlessness which results in impotence. This applies to both male and female.
3. Emotional need.
4. Self love
5. Sensation based sexuality

Where an emotional balance is sought

At this level you have the 'women who love too much' and those who fear commitment or need to be the centre of attention. Marilyn Monroe was stuck here. So too was Jack Kennedy, who was highly evolved, but the stuckness in this centre held everything back, so that he had to pass over.

6. This is where you offer emotional comfort because this is what you need.
7. This chamber moves you from nurturing in order to get something back – for example smother love or the parent who buys things for their offspring but expects love in return – to nurturing with love.
8. From insecurity about your sexuality to a sense of security.

The higher chambers, where there is no flip side

You are now on the ascension path and this chakra starts to glow. The caring and tenderness from this centre spills out into friendships. You start to look after others. An example of this is Bob Geldof who was drawn to help starving children.

9. Mutual caring.
10. Tenderness.
11. Offering love.
12. Giving love.

13. Sharing love.
14. Transcendent sexuality and love.
15. Procreation to bring in a child.
16. Carrying a baby with love. This also applies to fathers, aunts and uncles or extended family who are supporting.

The Navel Chakra

When this chakra becomes fifth dimensional it is a wonderful, warm, bright orange so that you feel friendly, warm, nurturing and sociable. You treat yourself and others with equal respect. You radiate serenity for this chakra becomes clear when you live in harmony with yourself and others. At this level Archangel Gabriel helps you to express your creativity and artistic abilities, appropriately.

There are sixteen chambers or petals in this chakra as there are in the Sacral chakra, which makes 32 chambers and the all encompassing one is the 33rd.

This is the journey of feelings and experiences for the ascension of this chakra:

The Chambers or Petals of the Navel Chakra

1. Isolation.
2. Withdrawal.
3. Aloofness.
4. Being afraid to move beyond your safe understanding, so that you have very tight boundaries and the opposite extreme of being totally unbounded.
5. Inability to relate.
6. Friendliness.
7. Reaching out and welcoming.
8. Warmth and caring.
9. Serving others and nourishing them emotionally, perhaps cooking for them.
10. Seeing the best in others.
11. Sociability.
12. Family.
13. Community.
14. Being inclusive.
15. Communal celebration.
16. Unconditional guidance and support.

The 33rd chamber is clairsentience.

Archangel Gabriel

A diamond is the materialised energy of Archangel Gabriel on Earth. It shines and glitters with light representing clarity, eternity, purity and love, which are the qualities of the great archangel. If you need clarity about your next step call on Archangel Gabriel to help you. His Orbs are seen wherever a person or place needs purification or support.

Wherever there are weddings, Archangel Gabriel will be present, supporting the intention of the couple.

His Orbs are often seen merged with angel of love. Together they precede masters and guides who are travelling to do a piece of work and clear the way for them.

You can always call on Archangel Gabriel for he can send one of his ten million angels to hold the light and cleanse a person or place. Wherever there has been negative energy, dirty deals, fighting, drugs, drinking or sadness, Archangel Gabriel's angels will be found, purifying the area. You can call his angels to help you or send them to somewhere that needs to be cleared. If you need to cleanse a space for spiritual work, invoke the mighty Archangel Gabriel.

Protection

Until I worked with Orbs I always asked Archangel Michael for protection and I still do. However I am very aware how much protection Archangel Gabriel confers. Where there is fear or negativity, he will arrive to purify the people or situation so that no danger can be attracted to their fear. Whenever I have photographed aeroplanes – usually a small dot in the sky – there are Archangel Gabriel's Orbs with it and sometimes all round it. They are much bigger than the plane.

When I photographed traffic wardens they too had Gabriel's Orbs with them!

Invocation for protection from Archangel Gabriel

Say clearly and with intention, 'I now invoke the mighty Archangel Gabriel to place a ball of his pure white, reflective light around me for my total protection. So be it. It is done.'

Then visualise the light bring placed round you and know that it is there. All negativity or lower frequencies will then bounce off you and will not be able to enter your aura.

Personal purification

If you are feeling, low, negative, grumpy, irritable, angry or hurting, it is a sure sign you need purification. One way is to call on Archangel Gabriel to fill you with his shimmering light. Breathe it in and accept it, allowing it to shine into every cell of your being.

Archangel Hope

If you are washing dirty clothes you expect them to be clean afterwards and this is the reward for your labours. So many people become despondent and forget to focus on the positive outcome they want. However big or small your task, Archangel Hope ignites a higher expectation within your consciousness.

A rainbow is the constant reminder of this. Rain accompanies this cascade of light. Of course a scientist will give you a valid scientific reason for this phenomenon but behind every scientific explanation there lies a spiritual cause. Whenever you see a rainbow you are being given a sign of hope orchestrated by Archangel Hope, with tiny elementals all doing their part.

Another example is the growth of flowers, who develop spiritually by expressing their beauty as well as their innate qualities. So a primrose represents modesty and quiet certainty; snowdrops purity and promise. They herald spring and the anticipation of new beginnings in those countries where there are seasons. Archangel Hope works with Archangel Purlimiek to encourage the elementals and fairies of these blooms to help these early flowers, especially when weather patterns are changing.

Chapter Thirteen

The Solar Plexus Chakra

This is the chakra of instinct, of gut feelings and reactions. It has great psychic antennae which reach out to check that your family and friends are safe. Its feelers are constantly moving to see that no cars are driving too close to you on the motorway or that you are not being cheated.

At the third dimensional level this chakra holds your deepest fears, which may well be unconscious but will nevertheless rule your life. If someone else with the same anxieties comes near you, your chakra will tense up. As you raise your frequency this chakra relaxes and your fears dissolve so you feel more tranquil and can spread a feeling of peace to others.

When you reach the fifth dimensional level you spread serenity and calm wherever you go. You feel contented and the wisdom you have gained in past lives becomes available to you once more. Then this chakra becomes deep gold with rainbow lights in it. Archangel Uriel, who is in charge of the angels of peace, helps with its evolution and development to enable you eventually to spread peace on Earth. When it is fully evolved you can connect with other star systems to spread goodwill.

There are thirty three chambers or petals in this chakra. Archangel Uriel assists by drawing negativity from your chakras so if you see one of his Orbs which is brown or murky, it has absorbed negativity and is taking it to the light to transmute.

Archangel Uriel also radiates divine light and wisdom from the chambers within his Orbs into your solar plexus. If you see one of his Orbs shining golden yellow, breathe the energy in as deeply as you can.

Every time you choose peace over conflict, calm over aggression or courage over cowardice you strengthen your solar plexus and Archangel Uriel connects more closely to you.

Petals or chambers of the solar plexus

1. Aggression or conflict.
2. Cowardice.

3. Fear of loss.
4. Anxiety or insecurity.
5. Imagining the worst.
6. Being a bully or a victim. These are opposite outcomes of the same belief.
7. Dependence or reliance.
8. Lack of self worth.
9. Lack of self esteem.
10. Lack of confidence.
11. Arrogance.
12. Lack of trust in people.
13. Lack of trust in life.
14. Suspicion.
15. Ego driven. You are driven to accomplish for personal gratification and desire for accolades.
16. Giving power away. You let others influence you or feel they are better than you are.
17. Accepting self.
18. Standing up for the rights of others.
19. Trusting others.
20. Independence.
21. Receiving love.
22. Trusting self.
23. Humility.
24. Inner peace.
25. Spreading peace.
26. Empowering others.
27. Sharing for the highest good. This is where people and communities become interdependent.
28. Harmless.
29. Healing your past lives.
30. Wisdom with the confidence it brings.
31. Bringing forward wisdom from your past lives.
32. Connecting with inter-galactic wisdom.
33. Being an inter-galactic master.

Archangel Uriel

Archangel Uriel with his twin flame, Aurora, is in charge of the development of the solar plexus chakra. The biggest thing that holds most people back from their spiritual journey is fear. When you have released old fears, the wisdom of your soul can come forward. Archangel Uriel will give you confidence and self worth to do whatever you need to do to further your ascension path. He directs the angels of peace and works through humans to bring unity and calm to the world.

When your solar plexus chakra becomes deep gold, filled with wisdom, you become a true ambassador for peace in the world.

In **picture (20)** the amazing Orb is Archangel Uriel himself with Archangels Raphael and Zadkiel, who have come to fetch souls in response to prayers for help. The Orb is full of people. They have come to take people who are frightened of dying and looking at this orb will help people to heal their fear of death, help people pass over, heal your solar plexus, heal any shock and trauma by enfolding you in love. Also when you look at this orb you will find depression lifting. Its main purpose is to send out international peace and an energy of reconciliation.

Archangels Uriel, Raphael and Zadkiel

When you look at picture (20) you receive a feeling of alignment with the universe.

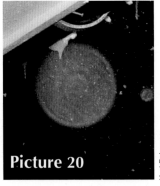

Picture 20

Kari Palmgren

Chapter Fourteen

The Heart Chakra

This chakra develops from self centeredness where your heart is closed to a centre of joyous, loving giving. At the third dimension it is green, the colour of nature and balance, with a pink centre. Because it is very connected with nature it is much easier for people to open the higher levels of the chakra when they can go out into a garden, park or the countryside. Walking on the land helps to drain all the tension from here, so that it can re-vitalise, relax and open again.

The emotions that block this centre and keep it closed, such as jealousy, envy, greed, guilt or meanness all arise from fear of lack and a belief that you are not lovable. They cause you to withhold love. People can sense the dirty green of jealousy or envy and are repelled by it.

Most of us have gone through pain, hurt and trauma, which we have not fully released, dealt with or forgiven. We tend to push this into the back of the heart chakra, where it energetically clogs the spine and prevents this centre from raising its frequency. On your journey to ascension it is time now to clear this.

The fifth dimensional heart chakra

At the fifth dimension the heart chakra is pure white, filled with Christ consciousness and aligned with the great cosmic heart. Then you totally love and accept, honour and respect all life forms and yourself.

Clearing the heart chakra

The first step to clearing and cleansing the old stuff from this important chakra is the desire and intention to do so. Make your decree clear that you are now ready to release the past and forgive everyone for anything they may have done to hurt you, deliberately or accidentally, consciously or unconsciously. Also that you are ready to forgive yourself for anything you may have done to hurt or harm another, consciously or unconsciously.

The second step is to love yourself. You are not part of your parents though you have come through them and they have provided the means for your entry and lessons for your spiritual growth. You are part of God. So if you love the Creator, you must love and accept yourself.

Stop asking what God can do to help you. Instead ask what the divine within you can do to help others.

Developing the qualities of higher love

These are empathy, compassion, self love and forgiveness. They all entail letting go of self and tuning into a higher perspective.

Empathy

Even if all that this person stands for is diametrically opposed to your notions, you merge yourself with them for the purpose of feeling with them. First open your heart, then place yourself into their heart and consciousness so that you can truly understand them. To do this you need to listen to them, really hear and feel their feelings as well as their views.

To practise this you might like to meld yourself for a few moments with a criminal, an extremist or someone with very different standards from yours. If this seems difficult or distasteful, pause and remember that we are all part of God and separation is caused by judgement. The sense of being judged causes people to feel bad and this is what makes them want to hurt others or behave inappropriately. As soon as you are prepared to suspend judgement and empathise with them, something deep within them shifts and they become lighter.

The good news is that high vibrations transmute lower ones, so if you meld yourself with Jesus, Krishna, Buddha, Mohammed or a saint their high consciousness lifts you. If you meld yourself with a person of dark consciousness, your lighter one starts to change them and, because of the quality of your intention, your heart rises in frequency.

Compassion

Like empathy, compassion means feeling with someone else, without judgement. It involves opening your heart and enfolding them with love. It offers a healing fifth dimensional energy.

Forgiveness

A closed heart arises when you withhold love because of something you perceive another has done to you. Forgiveness is about giving love no matter what has happened. Because this quality has such a high frequency, it heals the giver and the receiver.

Forgiveness enables spiritual energy to flow through the heart again and each cell to open once more like a flower. So it dissolves physical as well as emotional blocks.

Self Love

The qualities above involve seeing the God in another. Self love means recognising the God in yourself. It is not about vanity, conceit or arrogance, which arise from ego and delusion. It is the quiet, simple knowing that, with all your human foibles, your essence is divine. When you truly understand this the walls between you and others drop away, hurts have no impact and you become a true servant of the divine. This enables you to transcend lower limitations and achieve the previously unattainable. You can fully open your heart and ascend to a high frequency.

Petals or chambers of the Heart Chakra

There are thirty three chambers or petals in the heart chakra. As I have inferred the outer ones are green, then they become pink, then violet pink until those in the centre are pure white. They open to the sun or light of Source, little by little, like a rose.

In the first part of the journey your heart is closed.

1. Unkindness.
2. Being unfeeling or cold.
3. Feeling hurt or angry.
4. Jealousy.
5. Self absorbed.
6. Greed.
7. Withdrawal.
8. Loneliness
9. Withholding or meanness.
10. Being sad or unhappy.

Now the petals start to open.

11. Love for animals.
12. Love of nature.
13. Love for children.
14. Love for partner.
15. Love for family.
16. Love for others.
17. Love for self.
18. Empathy.
19. Compassion.
20. Caring.

21. Forgiveness of others.
22. Forgiveness of the entire Earth experience.
23. Forgiveness of self.
24. Warm hearted.
25. Welcoming.
26. Generous.
27. Unconditional giving.
28. Love for humanity.
29. Unconditional love.
30. Transcendent love.
31. Connection with the cosmic heart.
32. Cosmic love.
33. Oneness.

Picture 21

Kari Palmgren

Archangel Chamuel

Archangels Chamuel and Charity, who are in charge of the development of this chakra, pour the palest pink love over you. Look at picture (21) and breathe in the energy to your heart for it will enable you to take in fifth dimensional love frequency.

Archangel Chamuel's angels are often seen with the radiant pure white angels of love, and when you see them together it can take the frequency of your heart even higher.

Archangel Chamuel and an angel of love

When you look at Orb (21) you receive love and joy and a desire to share this with others.

Archangel Charity

St Francis said, 'It is in giving that we receive,' and Archangel Charity works with this spiritual law to help all those who give freely with an open heart.

Archangel Metatron

When you open your heart to Archangel Metatron, you accelerate your opportunity for ascension. For more about this mightiest of archangels, see Chapter 20.

Chapter Fifteen

The Throat Chakra

This chakra is turquoise at the third dimension, so it is blue mixed with green, requiring balance and the ability to communicate honestly. Every time you say what you truly feel instead of trying to please, impress or placate others the petals become clearer. Many third dimensional people use the excuse that they could not tell someone how they felt because it might hurt them. In fact they are protecting themselves from the imagined response of the other.

Falsehood, however well intentioned, strikes a discord in the unconscious of the person to whom it is spoken. Without understanding why, they feel uncomfortable or even fearful. People who are told well meaning half truths feel as if they are walking on shifting sands.

Truth has a resonance which aligns with your deepest knowing. Although it may not be what you want to hear, it gives you strength and you can move forward.

Janice and John were thirteen and ten years old. Their parents were not getting on but they prided themselves that they never quarrelled in front of the children. Nevertheless the atmosphere in the house was tense. 'Of course, they think everything is fine,' their mother told me. John was acting up, while Janice had become very quiet and withdrawn and watched everything with big wary eyes. 'It's just their age,' their mother said. When at last she told them that she and their father were having a trial separation she was surprised that Janice heaved a sigh of relief and said, 'At last.' John continued to misbehave but when he realised that he was being kept in the picture and told the truth, he too responded positively.

I heard another similar story where the father was very ill. Everyone kept reassuring his teenage daughter that he was going to get better and her mother pulled together all her reserves of strength to show a courageous face, though in her heart of hearts she knew her husband was dying. The girl became angry, insolent and disobedient, because she could sense she was being fed untruths. When, at last the mother confessed her fears and told her that her father was really desperately ill, the girl, though grief stricken, matured and became a solid support for her mother. Her honesty meant that her daughter trusted her and felt safe, however sad.

The throat chakra is very sensitive and at an unconscious level tunes into everything whether verbalised or not. It is connected to clairaudience. So if you pick up that someone is going to say something you do not want to hear, you tense up the back of your throat chakra. If you do this often enough, this centre will slow down or clog up.

There are twenty two chambers or petals in the throat chakra. When you go into them you take a journey to higher consciousness.

Chambers or Petals of the Throat chakra

When you work with this chakra you must start from the highest chamber and make your way backwards to the outer ones, because you need a high level of protection. If you enter from the lowest, entities could get in, so it is imperative to call in Archangel Michael's cloak when you are there. When you begin from the highest, as you address the lesson of each chamber, this automatically draws in protection and light which heals the earlier steps.

We were also told that those who are engaged with these higher levels need to send protection to those who are not yet at this stage. For example, there are television programmes which go to haunted places where it is dangerous to enter without protection. There are also mediums who are working with the uninitiated and it is vital that they make sure that those working with them are clear and protected.

As with all the chakras, you may have done some of the journey in past lives.

There are 22 stages.

22. Trust in God.
21. Trust in self.
20. Be an ambassador of light.
19. Inspired leadership with integrity.
18. Honouring your magnificence.
17. Teaching truths.
16. Speaking with honour and integrity.
15. Being open and aligned to the higher truth.
14. Speaking up for self.
13. Speaking up for others.
12. Knowing who you are.
11. Accepting your magnificence.
10. Speaking to empower others.

9. Telepathy.

8. Speaking the divine truth no matter what.

7. Being influenced to misrepresent the truth. This is often where you go along with others.

6. Fear of being misunderstood, disbelieved or persecuted.

5. Trusting your inner voice.

4. Listening and hearing.

3. Refusing to listen.

2. Deliberately telling falsehoods.

1. Lying or being dishonest to protect yourself.

The fifth dimension

As the frequency of this chakra rises more violet light enters. Then purple merges with it, bringing a little red for action. When this happens the chakra spins and radiates a magnificent royal blue, the colour of majesty, power and truth.

Then you are ready to work with Archangel Michael, to hold his sword of truth in your right hand and his shield of protection in your left. This symbolises that you are prepared to speak with integrity, honesty and tact for the highest good. You use your fine-tuned intuition to know what it is right to say. You also protect those who are weaker or less able to look after themselves than you are.

At this level you are a mighty warrior for the Truth.

Archangel Michael

Archangel Michael, one of the best known and loved archangels, rules this chakra. His angels are seen with many Orbs, their distinctive deep, radiant blue protecting other archangels, angels and spirits.

We are delighted to be able to show you two Orbs of Archangel Michael himself. I took the first one in Thailand during a rainstorm. With Archangel Uriel and many angels of love he was on his way to Bangkok to protect animals during a tropical cloudburst. He is radiating courage, strength and protection and bringing through Source energy. You can see the pure white centre where he is open to Source. Archangel Michael protects you as you aim for the spiritual heights and gives you the strength and courage to get there.

Picture 22

Diana Cooper

Archangel Michael

When you look at Orb (22) you will receive a great boost of courage, strength and protection.

***

Picture 23

Ann Marie Bentham

Archangel Michael transmitting to aspects of Archangels Gabriel and Uriel

When you look at Orb (23) you receive an unconscious confirmation that there are angels

In picture (23), taken by Ann Marie Bentham, the mighty Archangel Michael himself is in the middle, a small blue light above the stone. He is radiating courage to the white Orb, which is an aspect of Archangel Gabriel with an angel of love and a unicorn and to the yellow one, an aspect of Archangel Uriel.

You can see that the latter two archangel Orbs are elongated and wide open to receive Archangel Michael's energy.

Most Orbs are seventh dimensional, the frequency of the angels. There is an outer ring round each of the white and yellow Orbs and this is a frequency band holding the Orb at the sixth dimensional level. The reason is that more people can see them with their physical eyes when they are radiating at a sixth dimensional frequency and this is part of the plan to make humans more aware of angels. It is the next step forward.

Archangel Michael is giving these archangels courage and strength. This is because many humans send out fear when they see them physically and this can impact on the angels when they are open. This is partly because many people who see them will think they are space ships and there is currently a great deal of anxiety about extra terrestrial connection. If Archangel Michael surrounded them, they could not bring their frequency down into the sixth dimension.

So in this picture the two angels are wide open taking in Archangel Michael's strength before they close down and become Orbs again. Then they will travel at the lower frequency in order that more people will become aware of them. This is a new phase of archangel activity that is just starting, designed to help humanity become aware.

***

Archangel Faith

Archangel Michael's partner is Faith and a demonstration of this quality is required for the throat chakra to develop to its full potential. She will help you hold your light and integrity.

Look at picture (40) in which Archangel Faith is the shooting Orb on the left hand side. Lord Kuthumi and Master Imor are with her, bringing higher teachings to this part of the world.

Chapter Sixteen

The Third Eye Chakra

This chakra in the centre of the forehead is known as the centre of enlightenment. When it vibrates at a fifth dimensional level it becomes a clear crystal ball. Then it activates clairvoyance and divine wisdom. The light that radiates from here then gives mental healing to others, touches their essence and lifts their frequency. It also enables you to find clarity, so you can draw in an abundance of your heart's desire and also manifest materially.

Archangel Raphael and his twin flame, the great Universal angel, Mary, work through this chakra to give healing and abundance.

There are ninety six petals or chambers in the third eye chakra, so we are not entering them all. However I will take you on the journey through the seven veils which must be pulled aside as you journey into the centre of this chakra.

The seven levels of the third eye

1. *Illusion.* The truth is that there is only love and light for that is God's essence and therefore your own. Anything that tries to tell you of separation, war, hurt, superiority or lack of love is illusion. Angels of light are part of the oneness and only whisper oneness and love. You can, however, encounter temptations on the spiritual path which try to induce you to feel different or better than another. This illusion will stay with you until you embrace love again. Then you have passed the test of this chamber.

2. *Mental healing.* This is about focussing and directing your thoughts towards a person or situation with healing intention. You use the power of your third eye.

3. *Telepathy.* This is the ability to tune in to all the frequencies of humans, spiritual beings and angelic forces, so that you receive their communications on all levels.

4. *Creation.* You use the power of your thoughts and visions to create and manifest.

5. *Clairvoyance.* This is clear seeing with the inner eye.

6. *Abundance.* Moving beyond, as you give so you receive, you now have a knowing of divine abundance and are ready to accept it.

7. *Claircogniscence.* This is all knowing, or gnosis.

Mother Mary

I have always puzzled about Mother Mary. How could a being of the angelic realms have incarnated? I have repeatedly been told by the spiritual hierarchy that angels never take physical bodies, so it seemed one of those enigmas beyond my comprehension. Now, Archangel Michael has given an explanation to expand my awareness. I am sure there are further greater layers and levels of understanding to be revealed when I am ready.

I have written in other books that Mary was Ma Ra in Lemuria and Isis in Atlantis and Egypt. In one sense that is right but Archangel Michael has now given us a higher explanation.

Who is Mother Mary?

She is a universal angel, one of the highest ranking of all angels, who works in more than one universe. She carries the purest divine feminine light of compassion and empathy. Because of this she heals through pure love.

Archangel Raphael

Archangel Raphael is the twin flame of Mother Mary and in charge of the development of the third eye. Naturally she works through here but the highest expression of her healing comes through the heart centre.

Is it possible for an angel to incarnate?

No.

Did Mary bear Jeshua Ben Joseph who attained the name Jesus?

No. The great Master and High Priestess Isis physically bore Jesus and she was overlit by Mary. In all her incarnations Isis was guided by the divine Mother Mary, who melded into her consciousness.

About Isis

Isis is of the human hierarchy and originates from Venus. All beings from Venus work on the heart ray of pure love.

She incarnated in Lemuria as Ma Ra, clearly under the Mary ray, where she set up the Mystery Schools. In Atlantis she was one of the original High Priestesses of the Golden Times. Later she gave virgin birth to Horus. At the fall of Atlantis she returned and took her tribe to South America where they became the Aztecs, renowned for their magnificent art and their knowledge of the stars. The Aztec calendar began with the birth of Venus and calculations are based on advanced astronomical knowledge. At the start of the Piscean Age Isis incarnated as Mary where she gave Virgin birth to the man who was to become Christ.

A story

I was told this story by a friend who I will call Molly, who went to a workshop where they were each told to imagine they were an Egyptian God. My friend knew immediately that she was to be Isis. There was a pile of books on a table and she picked one randomly and opened it at a page of sayings by Isis, so she knew she was being guided.

Then they sat in a circle and shared their findings. When it was Molly's turn, she tuned in and was overshadowed by Isis who spoke through her. At the end her teacher stood and bowed to her (as Isis) but no one else. My friend stood and felt Isis in her as she bowed back in a way she would not normally have done.

One of the workshop participants was particularly touched by this. This lady had terribly disruptive neighbours, who complained whenever they mowed the lawn and about everything else. These neighbours also had constant barbeques where billows of smoke crossed her patio. This woman decided to ask Isis to help with the situation and from that day there were no more complaints from her neighbours and no more barbeques.

Mary's Orb on the back cover

Gillian Barnes kindly sent the magnificent Orb on the back cover of Mother Mary herself with Archangel Zadkiel, taken at Lourdes above the statue of the holy Mother on the 10th May, 2007 at about 3pm. This Orb is specifically for the opening of the soul star chakra and to heal the heart. There is more about it in Chapter 19.

Chapter Seventeen

The Crown Chakra

The chakra at the top of the head is known as the thousand-petalled lotus because of the thousand chambers or petals it contains, which resemble a water lily or lotus when it opens. Each of these is connected to an aspect of God.

The analogy is that the spiritual journey starts in the base, where a lotus has its roots in the mud of negativity. The bud of spiritual potential rises until it surfaces and opens its petals to the sun. In the case of a human our journey is from the mud of the base, up the chakras in the spine or stalk until the crown chakra opens. Then it is like a chalice which accepts light from the higher transpersonal chakras, which it filters down into the lower chakras.

Archangels Jophiel and Christine help this chakra to develop from violet at the third dimension to a transparent clear crystal. Jophiel brings in ancient wisdom and Christine holds the Christ light here.

The thousand petals of the crown chakra

These represent the thousand vibrational frequencies of God.

When I stayed in Amma's ashram in Kerala, one of the most profound experiences of each day was to rise very early to listen to the swamis chanting the thousand names of God. In doing this with intention they intoned the thousand frequencies of the crown chakra. It was always an awesome experience and the vibrations used to flow through me for hours. I always felt them open me up into a transcendent state.

Archangel Jophiel

Archangel Jophiel is in charge of the development of the crown centre, which is the chalice that collects energy from the transcendent chakras and passes it down through the body. He is the Archangel of Wisdom.

Archangels Jophiel, Metatron, Gabriel and Michael with Lady Nada

When you look at Orb (24) you receive help to develop your intuition and higher psychic and spiritual gifts.

Eugene McGill sent us the magnificent yellow Orb (24) in which Archangels Jophiel, Metatron, Gabriel and Michael are bringing Lady Nada to collect her mother as she ascends. This is a very high frequency Orb for Archangel Jophiel is bringing wisdom and also holding Lady Nada's wisdom, while Archangel Gabriel is purifying those who are looking at the Orb and receiving the energy. Archangel Metatron has come with this Orb to open you up to be ready to access your Stellar Gateway, while Archangel Michael is travelling with Lady Nada to protect her. She has come to help people of high integrity develop intuition and their higher psychic and spiritual gifts.

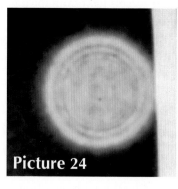

Picture 24

Eugene Mc Gill

Chapter Eighteen

The Causal Chakra

Between the crown and the soul star lies the shimmering white causal chakra representing the stillness and peace of the higher mind. This chakra also brings the light of your soul into your mental body and to enable this to happen you must open your right brain and regulate your left brain. Your right brain is your creative side, which sees expanded concepts and the whole picture. Your left brain contains your programmed beliefs and structured, learned concepts.

I have often seen unicorns working with this chakra to help it become quiet, still and open. When you can remain calm and peaceful during difficult times, messages or concepts from the spiritual realms can be received into it. When you have mastered your higher mind, often through meditation, you can receive stellar transmissions. Cosmic ideas planted here need quiet, time and space to grow and manifest.

When this chakra has received, digested and accepted information from above, it then transmits it to the cells of the body. Archangels Christiel and Mallory also bring the silence and stillness of the Christ energy to this spiritual centre. As more people are anchoring their causal chakras, the collective mental body of the planet is becoming purer and starting to hold the divine thought of God.

If you are helping others to develop stillness in this chakra, for example by teaching meditation, yoga, mind control or any other form of mental discipline, Archangel Christiel will bring appropriate masters to you to help you. See Orb (38) of Archangel Christiel bringing Babaji to a yoga class.

Right and left brain

Left-brain learning is logical, linear, rational, scientific, mathematical and ordered. A left brain dominant person tends to accept and repeat other people's ideas, for they often lack original thinking or creative ideas. Such individuals enforce rules and regulations and prefer to follow instructions. As a consequence their natural life spark becomes depressed and they may feel they lose their divine connection. If you recognise yourself as too left brain, take time each day to be quiet and listen to your still, quiet voice. Then carry any creative ideas forward.

The right brain is responsible for originality, creativity, imagination, rhythm, song, artistic ability, spiritual connection and an open heart.

You cannot ascend by using your left brain, for ascension is a right brain process. It requires creativity, devotion, open mindedness, expanded concepts and imagination within the third eye.

Nor can you use masculine energies of linear thinking, containment, force, pressure or strength, for ascension calls on feminine qualities of nurturing, kindness, love, empathy, compassion, sharing, acceptance, giving and an attitude of inclusion.

This is why so many men are developing their feminine side. It is also why so many males are incarnating as 'gay', so that they can experience and express their softer qualities.

Manifesting your vision

Writing utilises the left brain. When you draw, you use the right brain. To ensure that your entire mind computer is helping you create your vision, decide what you wish to manifest, write it down, then illustrate it.

Petals or chambers of the Causal Chakra

There is only one chamber, which is entry into the silence.

Archangel Christiel

Look at the Orb (38) of Christiel bringing Babaji to access the energy of peace and stillness of the higher mind (page 129).

Archangel Mallory

Archangel Mallory, the twin flame of Archangel Christiel, is bringing the divine feminine balance into the Causal chakra. The wonderful Orb in picture (25) is an angel of love with Archangels Mallory, Uriel and Michael carrying a spirit. The angel is radiating love to you as you look at the Orb.

As you evolve to a higher frequency you start to open up to your past lives in order to understand your soul's journey. Here Archangel Mallory is stimulating an interest in your past lives, while Archangel Uriel is helping you to access the wisdom you have accrued from them. Archangel Michael is protecting you as you explore them. At the same time he is protecting the spirit – a trainee guide – who is travelling in the Orb.

Archangels Christiel, Mallory and Zadkiel Orbs

We were sent by Outi Seppi truly awesome Orb pictures of Archangels Christiel and Mallory with other archangels and masters and she has very kindly given us permission to reproduce them. In picture (25) Archangel Mallory, the white Orb, is bringing spirits and is holding the energy. Archangel Zadkiel's violet light is encapsulating and protecting Archangel Mallory, who is bringing spirits to receive information and energy from the sun.

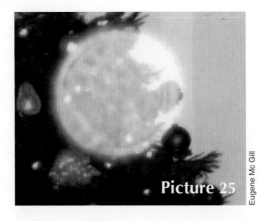

Picture 25

Eugene Mc Gill

Archangels Mallory, Uriel and Michael
with an angel of love and a spirit

When you look at Orb (25) you receive the desire to access your past life wisdom, the protection to do so and the wisdom to use it for your ascension pathway.

***

Picture 26

Outi Seppi

Archangels Christiel, Mallory and Zadkiel

When you look at picture (26) you receive exhilaration from Source

In picture (26) both the white Orb, which is Archangel Christiel and the magenta one, which is Archangels Mallory and Zadkiel merged, are receiving energy from the sun, which is connected to the Great Central sun and Source itself. This is bringing aspiration, inspiration and a feeling that you must succeed. It expands all your boundaries and is coming through now for the mass opening of the soul star chakra.

Chapter Nineteen

The Soul Star Chakra

Below the Stellar Gateway, a step down in vibration, is the eleventh chakra, the soul star chakra, which is magenta, for it holds the wisdom of the divine feminine. It accepts and assimilates the light from the ultimate chakra and filters it into the soul if you are ready. The soul star prepares you to open to unconditional love. Here the angels help you to balance your masculine and feminine aspects for true mastery.

In order to open and activate the soul star you must practise psychic cleansing and clear out mental negativity in the area. This is where your discordant thoughts and beliefs crystallise and these need to be swept away. Many of these come from our ancestors, for beliefs and patterns are carried forward as family karma. For example if your father believed he would never be able to support his wife and children, he would manifest this by being inadequate as a provider. If he never changed this belief you or one of your siblings will *at some level* take it on.

This may manifest differently from your father for your fear of being like him or your determination to prove yourself may cause you to drive yourself to success. However the source of the driving force will be a family fear held in your soul star chakra.

Future generations will undertake any family karma you have not dealt with, so if you have no children, others in your genetic line will undertake it. In the same way if you had aunts or great aunts, uncles or great uncles, who had no issues, the family karma may funnel down through you.

To clear this chakra:

1. Ground yourself. Black tourmaline placed on the floor at your feet will ground you.
2. Call in Archangel Zadkiel to transmute any negativity with his Violet Flame. Picture it happening.
3. Then visualise a golden-white ball of energy radiating in your soul star chakra.

4. Ask the unicorns to help you purify this chakra of all unhelpful ancestral and collective belief systems.
5. The crystal selenite can be used to help you clear and raise the frequency of the soul star.

It is very easy to taint this delicate chakra. Any unhealthy thought, projection or image you hold can bring the vibration down. So can the use of drugs, the churning of angry thoughts or lower astral travel.

Archangels Zadkiel and Amethyst

They are twin flames, helping to transmute the old energies of the first chamber of this centre with violet light, so that this chakra is prepared to accept light from Source.

You must go through this first chamber before you can access the inner one.

Archangel Zadkiel

When you look at picture (27) you receive energy which propels you to action for the highest good.

Picture 27

Dawn Gilroy Smith

The glorious Orb in picture (27) is Archangel Zadkiel himself. He is enhancing the beauty of this lovely place so that those who walk here feel joy, as do you when you look at the picture. It gives you vitality and life force.

**

Archangels Mariel and Lavender

Archangel Mariel represents the higher chamber of this chakra and he carries the masculine energy. He is closely linked with Mother Mary and is upholding the magenta flame.

His twin flame Archangel Lavender brings in the divine feminine aspect. She carries High Priestess energy and has a very special task. As her name would suggest she is involved with the purification of the soul star and this she relays through all the chakras, down to the Earth Star and up to the Stellar Gateway.

She also helps you to heal your soul star during your sleep. Because this chakra is very connected to family, ancestral and collective karma, she protects you from the energy of those ancestors who are unhelpful to your progress. At the same time she communicates with all your past family, helping with any forgiveness that is needed, giving wisdom to them and offering them permission to share their wisdom with you.

Angels of Archangels Mariel, Lavender and Chamuel

When you look at the Orbs on the front cover you receive a joyous awakening of your heart and your stellar gateway

We were sent a wonderful Orb of angels of Archangels Mariel and Lavender, who are receiving light. They are also carrying spirits to enjoy the experience. When you send the light from your heart upwards to your soul star chakra, it shines more brightly, which in turn wakens your stellar gateway. So as you look at the picture on the front cover breathe into your heart and send energy up and out of your stellar gateway.

**

Mother Mary and Archangel Zadkiel Orb

This awesome Orb on the back cover was taken by Gillian Barnes on 10th May 2007 where the apparition of our Lady, the Virgin Mary appeared for the first time in the grotto in Lourdes, France. In it Archangel Zadkiel has merged with Mother Mary and the Divine Mother herself came in to talk to us as we explored this picture. She said that as you look at this Orb it helps you to awaken, open and activate your soul star chakra. It also links you to Chiron and Vesta to help heal your heart. Chiron is the wounded healer and Vesta the mother of the home.

When people visit a place where she has appeared, like Lourdes or Fatima, with pure intention, just being in the energy of the place helps them to open this spiritual centre. This is because she has set the appropriate vibration by appearing there.

There is to be a mass opening of people's soul star chakras in the near future which is why this Orb is so important.

Mother Mary and Archangel Zadkiel

When you look at the Orb on the back cover you receive an invitation to walk the journey of the heart chakra with Mother Mary's help and a direct link to Mother Mary's heart and the cosmic heart.

∗∗∗

Alison Chester-Lambert, who is an astrologer, kindly sent me a detailed and fascinating article she wrote about the astrology of this Orb. I have only the space to pass on a condensed version of her wisdom.

The original appearance in Lourdes of Our Lady was on 11th February, 1858, which can be considered a beginning or `birth` in astrology. A chart or horoscope drawn up for that day will show what her appearance is for. According to Alison **the `birth chart` of Our Lady says her destiny and purpose is very much about human compassion, forgiveness, loving and healing in the energy of the Universal Mind of God. The original message of Our Lady is wake up!**

When Alison compared the horoscope of Our Lady with a chart of the planets for the time the photograph was taken she could instantly see an extremely strong link between the first appearance of Our Lady and the Orb in May. **The astrology of the Orb suggests that it is a wake up call!** She said that on the day the Orb photograph was taken, 10th May 2007, Jupiter and Uranus were moving into a relationship with each other that results in an action. They were causing each other to DO something. In astrology, when Uranus is involved in an event we can expect a sudden revelation, awakening or enlightenment. Uranus can liberate our deepest wishes. Jupiter delivers potency and confidence. He is associated with guardian angels, protection, confidence and empowerment. He sees the vision and potential of something and urges `go for it`. When he is involved we have no worries, we feel wrapped in divine benevolence. We trust and we just KNOW, as in Gnosis. **Astrology says Mary was released to her purpose in May 2007. We are so blessed to see this Orb.**

***

Alison Chester-Lambert drew my attention to another Orb taken on the same day and in the same position above Mother Mary's statue, as the Mary and Archangel Zadkiel Orb. I looked at it on her website and saw that it was Archangel Gabriel with the Master Hilarion. The message they brought was, 'Wake up to the fact that we have created the possibility of Orbs.' They added that when you go somewhere to take a photograph with spiritual intention, if you draw in an Orb, it enhances the results of your intention.

***

Just before we were asked by Kumeka and the angels to write the Orb books, Diana went to Fatima with two master teachers from the Diana Cooper School for the express purpose of being in the Mary energy. We found the energy in the main square of Fatima very disappointing but when we eventually found Mother Mary's statue in the olive groves, we could truly feel her light round us. After the visit, Archangel Michael said that we were sent there to help our soul star chakras receive her divine light.

Before you open your soul star chakra there is a journey involved. First you must have the right intent and consciousness to reach this chakra and must work with Archangel Zadkiel and in the ways described above in 'To clear this chakra' to prepare it. When you arrive at this level you may think you have done the work and that your soul star is fully open. However this is only the beginning.

After you have cleansed and prepared the first stage, you move into a space of reflection before you can reach the next gateway. This enables you to enter the higher level of the soul star where you access the Mary Orb and Archangel Mariel. He helps you develop the feminine aspect of this chakra.

In the space between the two reflect on your love for your family, humanity, the world and yourself. Then your karma is completed because you love and value yourself so you can value others. Loving yourself is the key to accessing this Orb and just looking at it opens the possibility of loving yourself more. Then you begin your journey to access Mary and the divine feminine. At this point many feel disconnected and in limbo. Suddenly life is not working as it did so you may give up.

If you can see this Orb, it will give you the impetus to continue.

Within this Orb there are 33 gates to different sections. Passing through these is the entry to Christ consciousness and to the cosmic heart. The journey entails entering every gateway for each one expands your level of love. These are the stages of opening your heart until you love humanity as a whole.

As you can see, the life of any parent takes them automatically through these opportunities. If you do not have children of your own you can follow this path with someone else's child or an animal. You may even do it with service, for example as a nurse or doing charity work. You may have learnt these lessons in a past life and not need to re-learn them in this one, which is why some childless people or even children themselves have soul star chakras that are fully operational. The opportunity for this is available to everyone.

Doorway 1   Loving yourself

Doorway 2   Loving your parents.

Doorway 3   Loving animals.

Doorway 4   Loving your siblings, cousins or close family.

Doorway 5   Loving your teenage self.

Doorway 6   Offering loving service to others.

Doorway 7   Loving your manhood or womanhood.

Doorway 8   Loving yourself through being in love.

Doorway 9   Making someone else happy.

Doorway 10   Loving your parents for all they have done to bring you to this stage.

Doorway 11   Loving service to a soul you are bringing in or to children you can have an influence on.

Doorway 12   A new level of loving yourself.

Doorway 13   Loving the new soul (the baby).

Doorway 14   Loving your partner deeply.

Doorway 15   Loving learning to be a parent.

Doorway 16   Learning to let the child love other people.

Doorway 17   Appreciating the grandparents.

Doorway 18   Spreading your love outside your family.

Doorway 19   Learning to nurture self.

Doorway 20   Love the difference between your child and other people's children.

Doorway 21   Trust your child with others.

Doorway 22   Trust others with your child.

Doorway 23   Re-establish yourself in the community.

Doorway 24   Work in harmony with your partner.

Doorway 25 Caring for your parents.

Doorway 26 Be happy.

Doorway 27 Let your child be more independent.

Doorway 28 Accepting yourself as you grow older.

Doorway 29 Love who you are.

Doorway 30 Love other people as they are.

Doorway 31 Setting your child free.

Doorway 32 Setting your parents free.

Doorway 33 Your spiritual growth.

Chapter Twenty

The Stellar Gateway Chakra

The Stellar Gateway, which is one to two feet, (30-60 cms.) above your head, is pure gold. It holds your monadic energy and contains the sum total of all your experiences. Your monad is your original divine spark and is the true essence of who you are. As you become ready to bring this higher energy down into your daily life, you simultaneously access Source energy. You experience ultimate consciousness – true oneness. You have to earn this right through spiritual endeavour and dissolution of ego, usually over many lifetimes.

Two Archangels oversee this chakra – Archangel Metatron who is helping the whole of humanity to rise in frequency and Seraphina, a Seraphim, who is forming the link with your monad and Source.

This chakra is the gateway to Source and is the most wonderful deep gold colour. When your lower chakras are ready this mighty flower opens so that you can access divine energy. Then it is a chalice which fills with holy nectar and filters it down to those below.

Archangel Metatron

Archangel Metatron is in charge of the development of the Stellar Gateway, the ultimate or twelfth chakra. In the Kabbalah this is known as the pinnacle of the Tree of Life, which is the sphere of Kether, the Crown. He is one of the most important angels in the hierarchy and one of the few beings who is allowed to look at the face of God, which is why he is often referred to as Prince of the Countenance.

In Greek the name Metatron comes from the words Meta and Tron, meaning beyond the matrix. Hence he is known as the servant of God, the Heavenly Scribe who transmits the daily orders of Source to Archangels Gabriel and Sammael as well as all the other archangels, in a way that they can be passed on to the angelic hierarchy. His Latin name is Matator, meaning a guide or measurer, because he brought through Sacred Geometry from Source. He is one of the angels that led the people of Israel out of the wilderness after their exodus from Egypt.

Archangel Metatron's Orb
Archangel Metatron and an angel of love

When you look at Orb (28) you receive an invitation to the ascension pathway

His Orb is deep gold with such life force and vitality that it appears bright orange. It is absolutely glorious. Every time I see one of his Orbs I am awed. When Patti McCullough's mother died, the angels appeared over the hammock where she loved to lie. Orb (28) is just one of them. It is Archangel Metatron himself and

Picture 28

Patti McCullough

you can see the different layers of his being from orange to gold, with a pure white angel of love in the middle.

***

Archangels Metatron and Sandalphon

Archangels Metatron and Sandalphon are twin flames, the alpha and omega, working with the first and the twelfth chakras, the highest and the lowest.

What is the connection between Archangel Metatron and the Prophet Enoch?

Enoch was a pious teacher, scribe, psychic and leader of his people. As a wise and highly evolved human he was overlit by Archangel Metatron. Through Metatron, Enoch channelled the 22 Hebrew letters and the original Tarot.

On one occasion two angels took him to observe the seventh and many other dimensions. He was also given divine instructions and wrote three hundred and sixty-six books. Then God revealed divine secrets to him, including that of Creation, the duration of time the Earth will survive and what will happen afterwards. After this experience he lived for thirty days, during which time he was able to instruct many people in all that he knew. Then he ascended and became the master who keeps the akashic records of the Jewish race, overseen by Archangel Metatron and Seraphina.

Archangel Metatron overlit Enoch to such an extent that many people saw him illuminated and believed he had become the archangel. It was because Metatron accessed Enoch through his *heart* centre that people believed he was the archangel himself.

Archangel Metatron and Thoth Hermes

Thoth, the great priest avatar of Atlantis, was known as the Egyptian Scribe, for he keeps the akashic records of the Egyptian races and all the Arab countries, overseen by Archangel Metatron. He still does this.

Enoch and Thoth are working together to try to bring peace between the Jews and the Arabs.

Archangel Metatron and Serapis Bey

Serapis Bey, who originated from Venus, is the Master of the Fourth Ray of Harmony and Balance. Like Thoth he was a priest avatar in Atlantis and Keeper of the White Flame. Now he is often known as The Egyptian because at the fall of Atlantis he worked with Archangel Metatron and his angels to influence the building of the Pyramids, where his teachings are hidden at a fourth dimensional level. As soon as enough people have raised their frequency sufficiently, they will be accessed. That will then bring the possibility of peace on Earth.

Archangel Metatron's universal cube

The geometric plan for your ascension and that of Earth. I had often seen pictures of Metatron's cube and switched off at the sight or mention of geometry, which is surprising as I studied under Pythagoras. Nevertheless it is true. Now that Kumeka has explained to us about the energy of it I find it fascinating. The diagram below is a simple version of the connection of the chakras, the archangels and planets, aligned for Earth's ascension. Picture (29) shows the diagram in colours given to us by the spiritual hierarchy.

The centre of everything is the heart, which is pure white at the cosmic levels of love. This is the key and holding point of all the energies. In fact, if you imagine lifting the heart circle so that it becomes the pinnacle, you create a six sided pyramid, into which comes the light of Source. Then the energy moves into the chakras and down to the outer circles consisting of the universal angels Seraphina and Roquiel and the four planets.

These are depicted in Archangel Metatron's energy colour of orange. They are also linked at an earthly level by green connections. The inner rectangle links the chakras, while yellow gold lines form the six pointed star, which creates the balance between heaven and Earth. And energy from the outer circles merges in the heart.

When you look at the coloured universal Metatron Cube (29) you receive keys to ascension.

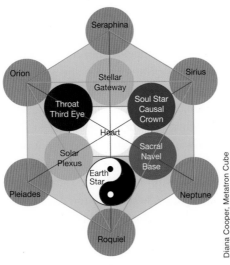

Diana Cooper, Metatron Cube

Here is the colour key.

Seraphina, Roquiel, Sirius, Orion, Pleiades, Neptune	Orange.
Stellar gateway	Sparkling gold.
Earth star	Black and white, yin yang symbol.
Throat, third eye chakras	Royal blue.
Solar plexus chakra	Gold.
Sacral, navel and base chakras	Platinum.
Soul star, causal and crown chakras	Magenta.
Heart chakra	White.
Lines of the six pointed star	Yellow gold.
Inner rectangle from centre of four chakras and below the stellar gateway and above the earth star	White with a hint of blue.
Lines linking the outer six orange spheres	Green.
Lines linking the centre of Seraphina to the centre Roquiel, centre of Neptune to centre of Orion and centre of Sirius to centre of the Pleiades through the heart	Violet.
Background	Pale yellow gold.

Archangel Metatron focuses on peace
Archangel Metatron with an angel of love

When you look at picture (30) you will receive universal peace in your heart.

This stunning golden Orb is Archangel Metatron with an angel of love, and you can see the pure white energy pouring out of it and also from the angel of love.

Many people are angry about war. In fact we all need to be at peace about peace. The message of this picture is, be the message of peace. Change yourself so that others will listen, for when you are at peace others will follow suit.

When Mother Theresa was asked if she would sign a petition against war, she said she would not but she would sign a petition for peace.

Here Archangel Metatron is bringing peace and wisdom to the heart, while the angel of love is imparting love, so that you too can radiate out love and peace, thus starting a ripple effect to change the world.

Picture 30

Alec Turner

***

Seraphina

Seraphina is a Seraphim, who vibrates on every colour. She works with Archangel Metatron at the Stellar Gateway and is the feminine counterpart to his masculine, touching aspirants with the divine feminine and a knowing of Oneness. She helps them to connect to the Seraphim, who are of the highest rank of angels surrounding the Godhead.

She also assists in the preparation of the Stellar Gateway, then builds and fine tunes the energy to it from Source. She even holds your hand as you climb the ladder to the Ultimate. Those who do so and connect directly with Source hold that frequency on Earth. They act as high frequency antennae, who tune into and broadcast that programme. This is a mighty task.

However these are not her main tasks. She has created a stepping stone between the Stellar Gateway and Source. The point where the star systems meet is like a great crystal ball and you can access it after you have awakened your Stellar Gateway. This gives some souls opportunity for greater divine service. Then, while part of you connects with Source, you are also invited to take on an Earth Ambassador role. At this stepping stone, within the crystal ball, she holds a training programme enabling those who are ready to undertake this mission. When you accept the invitation to enter this space you open to another dimension and she enlightens you.

The crystal ball is an entry portal to places in the universes that a person needs to access. For example both Kathy and I come from the same planet and we can only access it through this portal.

Chapter Twenty One

Etheric Retreats of the archangels

*Sandalphon	Magical crystal cave in Guatemala, Central America.
Roquiel	Uluru, Australia.
Joules	Deep in the ocean in the middle of the Bermuda Triangle.
Gabriel	Mount Shasta, California, which is in the Rockies.
Hope	Malaya.
Uriel and Aurora	Tatra Mountains, Poland.
Chamuel and Charity	St. Louis, Missouri. Charity is further inland along the Mississippi.
Michael and Faith	Banff, Canada.
Raphael	Fatima, Portugal.
*Mary	Lourdes, France.
Jophiel and Christine	South of the Great Wall, China.
Christiel	Not from Earth. Steps down through the Pleiades and enters through Jerusalem, which is his retreat.
Mallory	Not from Earth. Steps down through the Pleiades and enters through Bethlehem, which is his retreat.
Zadkiel and Amethyst	Cuba.
Mariel and Lavender	The Himalayas.
*Metatron	Comes from Orion and steps down through Luxor, which is his retreat.
Seraphina	Steps down through Neptune. No specific place to access this Seraphim.
Fhelyai	The Holy Island, Scotland.
Purlimiek	The Great Zimbabwe, Africa.
*Butyalil	Steps down through the Pyramids. His retreat is above Earth in the central point where the four ascension stars Neptune, Pleiades, Orion and Sirius, meet.
Gersisa	In Hollow Earth, right in the core of the Earth.

*There are seven important retreats to visit for ascension.

1. Archangel Sandalphon at the magical crystal cave in Guatemala.

   Here Sandalphon will nurture the seeds of your potential for this life. He helps with the opening of your Earth Star and Stellar Gateway. He also links you to your Monad or I AM Presence, your original divine spark.

2. Mother Mary at Lourdes.

   Mother Mary helps you connect with the cosmic heart and she expands your personal heart to open with compassion and love. She helps you connect with the unicorns and fairies.

3. Archangel Metatron at Luxor.

   Metatron expands your understanding of ancient wisdom. He is a catalyst for bringing all the planets into the right place for ascension. This is a mighty undertaking and he will give you a task if you come here.

4. Lord Voosloo at Stonehenge.

   He connects you to the highest and deepest wisdom of Atlantis and helps to bring back your 12 strands of DNA.

5. Archangel Butyalil at the Pyramids.

   Butyalil strengthens your cosmic links and connects you with the mighty Seraphim, Seraphina. He also links you to the Intergalactic Council, so that you can personally present petitions for the betterment of humanity and the cosmos or you can request help with a scheme.

6. Lord Meitreya at the Confucius Temple, China.

   You may ask Meitreya to overlight you with Christ consciousness and open you up to carry more of this light. You can ask him to place it in your solar plexus to reduce fear and replace it with empowerment and peace.

7. Lord Melchizedek at Guam, Vietnam

   Here you will receive cosmic teachings from Lord Melchizedek and learn how to spread it. He enables you to speak in a way that others can hear it.

Chapter Twenty Two

Archangel Azriel

Archangel Azriel has had a 'bad press' because he is the angel of death who is always there to collect someone when they pass. Like all other archangels he can send out millions of aspects of himself wherever he is needed. He comes with love and compassion to ease and supervise the passing and to try to ensure that every soul is met by their loved ones.

Because humans have free will, he cannot make a soul move towards the light as they leave the body. Some are in shock and cannot see the angels, others may have taken substances that prevent them from seeing the light and they need prayers to help them. Nevertheless one of Archangel Azriel's angels will be holding the light.

We were sent an extraordinary Orb of Archangel Azriel himself, with many archangels, carrying hundreds of souls as they passed. The archangels had been to a disaster scene and collected an entire group soul as they died, plus many others not of that group.

A group soul is a cluster of people on the same soul vibration who may not necessarily know each other while in physical life. They choose to pass together to clear something on passing and it is a combination of their energy that makes the clearance happen. Occasionally their passing together is considered such a tragedy that it creates change on Earth. Preparations are always made in advance to collect the group soul together and to receive them onto the other side.

Archangels Azriel, Raphael, Uriel, Gabriel, Michael, Zadkiel, Mariel, Metatron and Chamuel taking hundreds of souls to the light

When you look at Orb (31) you receive a knowing that you are looked after when you die.

Archangel Azriel is yin yang, black and white. In picture (31) he is black because he has absorbed all the emotions of those who have died in the disaster. Archangel Michael has come to protect everyone. Archangel Raphael is giving them all heal-

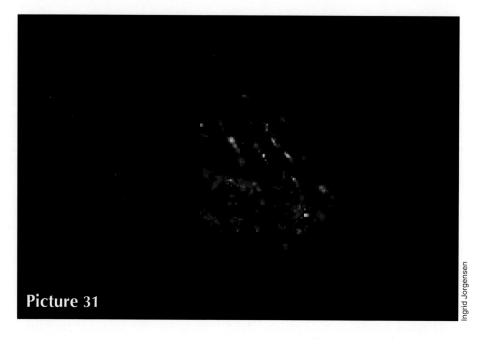

Picture 31

Ingrid Jorgensen

ing. Archangel Uriel is holding them in peace. Archangel Gabriel is purifying the situation. Archangel Chamuel is surrounding the souls in love. Archangel Zadkiel is transmuting their fears. Archangel Mariel is helping those who are almost ready to ascend, to raise their frequency that little bit higher. Archangel Metatron is helping those who are ascending. It helps these souls to die together and be collected at the same time for it offers them a sense of safety.

Section Three

Ascended Masters

Chapter Twenty Three

The Ascended Masters

Those who have incarnated on Earth and learnt all the lessons of this plane of existence become ascended masters. Once they have conquered that particular spiritual mountain their soul can, after their passing, choose to help those still on the climb – or they may decide to focus on different work. If they sign on to help those on the ascension pathway, first they train on the inner planes with great masters like Dwjhal Kuhl and Lord Kuthumi, the World Teacher. Then they are ready to assist the humans that are in the process of ascension. Because a wave of people are expected to ascend in the next hundred years, there are currently many of these new, recently trained, ascended masters on the other side, watching our progress and waiting to reach down a hand to help us.

There are also great, experienced ascended masters of enormous stature available to assist us. Some like Joshua Ben Joseph, who attained the name of Jesus and carried the Christ conscious energy for humanity at that time, incarnated into several bodies throughout the ages and ascended each time.

All the lessons of ascension are to do with integration of the higher qualities, especially love.

How can the ascended masters help your ascension?

When you think about an ascended master you automatically make a link which calls them to you. The more you read about them, meditate with or invoke them, the closer you become to them. You may feel yourself very drawn to one or you may connect with several of them.

When you make a connection the ascended master can help you in various ways:

1. They can telepathically impart divine information and light to you.
2. They enable you to access more energy of the ray or rays they work with.
3. You can receive teaching or healing from them when you attend their inner planes retreats during your sleep.

4. They can encourage your spiritual progress and enhance the qualities you need.

5. They can act as guides.

6. Just as you have one archangel who oversees your journey, you have a senior master who undertakes the same role. You can communicate with your master and, if you form a strong, mature relationship with them, it will greatly assist your progress.

7. Your guides consult the highly evolved masters about the best way to help your spiritual progress. Then they will open doors, arrange meetings and synchronicities that will create the right possibilities for you.

Chapter Twenty Four

The 12 Rays

The divine white light from God is divided into colour rays, which shine onto Earth. All colours affect us, as we know from the way in which we describe our moods. One person may be in a black mood. Another may feel blue. Someone will be in the pink and their friend will be in a golden glow. Golden sunlight brightens us up, while the silver moon makes us feel more reflective. If you need energising you may choose to wear red or orange.

Colour breathing, where you look at a colour and breathe it in to cellular level is recognised as a potent form of healing. It is even more effective to sit with a specific colour light shining onto you. Colour rays of the Source light influence you deeply and profoundly for each one bathes you with specific divine energy. A rainbow is the visible manifestation of this Source light.

At the time of Golden Atlantis where the vibration was the highest and purest it has been since Earth began, there were twelve rays pouring their influence onto humanity.

The five master rays carried a divine charge between 8,500 and 22,000 cycles per second. As Atlantis devolved these five highest frequency rays were withdrawn because their immense power was misused. At last these master rays have been restored to us, albeit at the lower end of their frequency range. We are now considered mature enough to use them for the benefit of humanity so the last one was reinstated in 2003.

The availability of the twelve rays greatly assists the ascension potential of millions of people, for as you access them, you are no longer a 60 watt light in the world. You become a floodlight who can light up the lives of the masses.

12 strands of DNA and 12 chakras

The withdrawal of the five master rays at the decline of Atlantis coincided with the closing down of five of the twelve chakras. 44 codons within the DNA were also sealed so that the twelve strands of DNA were reduced to two.

As part of the ascension of the planet, this is to be reversed until everyone once more has twelve operational chakras and twelve strands of DNA, for these are intimately connected.

The Masters of the 12 rays

In the following chapters I list the masters of the twelve rays, all of whom are ascended masters, though they have not necessarily earned their ascension from this planet. They are all extraordinary, wise and powerful beings, who have undertaken many awesome responsibilities during their lives and since they left this plane of existence. Yet they can all empathise with you and understand you as a human being.

Chapter Twenty Five

Ray 1 – El Morya

Ray 1 is a beautiful clear red vibration, and brings vitality and life force to your journey. Red is the colour of the spiritual warrior. It is often known as the ray of power, will or purpose and is about using your divine will rather than your lower will. It also involves using your integrity and not allowing another to influence you. This is a ray of action and some red is always merged with the higher colours when active leadership is required.

For example, royal blue, the colour of empowered communication has red in it, as does purple, which is the colour of leadership. Archangel Metatron, in charge of the Stellar Gateway, merges red into gold and his Orb is a beautiful, luminous orange. When he is taking action, he sends out the red aspect of himself. See picture (28).

Those of lesser understanding who are under this ray's influence may use its force to be domineering or to bully, control or fight others. To become an initiate of this ray, you are required to practise self discipline, use your power for the highest good, protect those who are in need or defenceless and lead by example. Most of all you must stand in your power. When you become a master of this ray you must take action to carry out the divine plan.

Military people, athletes or sports people of any kind, commanders, heads of corporations, spiritual leaders are often influenced by this ray. If it rules their personality they may be ruthless in their drive and ambition but if they have overcome this and act from their soul, they will move mountains for the highest good.

El Morya

El Morya is the Chohan or master of the first ray and he co-operates with Archangel Michael, the archangel who actively protects people and animals on Earth.

El Morya originates from Mercury but is working very closely with Earth to help with ascension. He is a member of the White brotherhood. He is soon expected to become The Manu, the perfected man, on which the new root race of humanity, the sixth root race, will be based. His chakras and energy fields will carry the qualities and characteristics of the next spurt of human evolution, so he will have twelve strands of DNA, be able to connect with cosmic wisdom and will stand as an example to all.

El Morya's past incarnations

As a priest in Atlantis he had advanced astrological and astronomical knowledge, which he took to the Euphrates at the fall. Then, as Abraham, he founded the Jewish religion.

He was Melchior, one of the Three Wise Men, all of whom were highly evolved and trained Magi. It was his advanced knowledge of the stars which enabled them to pin point the time and place of Jesus' birth so that they arrived in time for the 'lying in'.

El Morya was the first to learn that water is more than a cleanser and purifier, that it has cosmic powers of transmutation. As a result he developed the understanding of baptism. With Lord Kuthumi, who was another of the Wise Men,

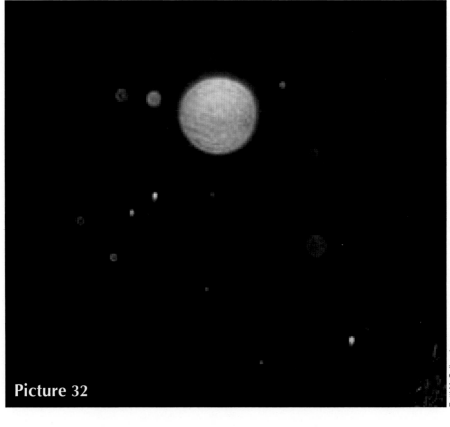

Picture 32

Patti McCullough

he influenced Madam Blavatsky to develop the Theosophical Society. He also incarnated as Akbar the Great, King Solomon and King Arthur, all of whom were revered for their wisdom.

Archangels Michael and Gabriel with a unicorn and El Morya

When you look at Orb (32) you receive an invitation to go to El Morya's etheric retreat

The stunning big orb (32) is of Archangels Michael and Gabriel and a unicorn, carrying El Morya to teach high frequency people about being prepared for 2012. When you visit the master's etheric retreat you will receive help to make sure you act from the divine will rather than your ego.

***

Abraham

After seeing an extraordinary dragon Orb we wanted to know more about them. Abraham came to answer our questions because, we then learnt, he works with them. We will be writing more about dragons in our book *Elemental Orbs*. His communications opened up a whole new world to me for I knew nothing about them and what wonderful beings they are.

It was while he was incarnated as Abraham that he founded and set up the Jewish religion and subsequently he has influenced their evolution. He will follow through with this mission by helping them to integrate with other races, for their learning is now almost complete.

Abraham's spiritual teacher was Melchizedek and he became a High Priest in the Order of Melchizedek, as was Jesus. Melchizedek is the title given to one who is initiated into this Order, which holds the Christ energy and the ancient wisdom for this universe.

Archangels Zadkiel, Raphael, Michael, Gabriel and Uriel with Abraham

When you look at Orb (33) you receive a downloading of ancient universal wisdom

Archangel Michael has merged with this Orb to protect the Master Abraham, Archangel Zadkiel is ensuring their journey is safe by transmuting any negative energy through which they pass. Archangel Raphael is sending out healing to those who look at the Orb and preparing your third eye to receive information and helping you to access your ancient wisdom. Archangel Gabriel is purify-

ing you, so that you are ready to receive the ancient wisdom from the Order of
Melchizedek which Abraham is bringing to impart to you.

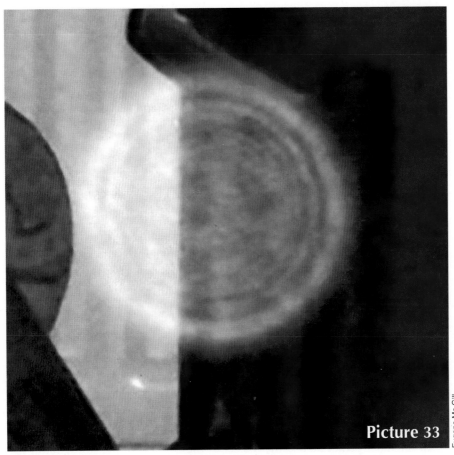

Picture 33

Eugene Mc Gill

Chapter Twenty Six

Ray 2 – Lanto

Ray 2 is a deep blue and yellow, for both colours represent different aspects of it. It is known as the ray of love, understanding and wisdom. Those who are influenced by this ray are learning to be loving, caring, compassionate and wise, and to teach these qualities to others.

If your lower personality is influenced by this ray you could be self centred, withholding both information and love. But when your soul is gloriously attuned to its higher vibration, you will be a great teacher, ambassador, illuminated spiritual teacher, counsellor or perhaps a creative but structured artist, such as an architect or photographer. You will be highly intuitive and able to think clearly and logically.

If you are working with the deep blue aspect you will seek opportunities to teach, heal, counsel and spread understandings. Under the yellow influence you will illuminate others with wisdom, creativity and joy.

Master Lanto

Lanto, the great Chinese philosopher, has now become master of this ray. He lived about 400 BC and is said to have spread more Christ light than any other master on earth. In his final incarnation he brought God so powerfully through his heart centre that people could see golden light shining from it. He is guardian of the golden flame and brought the wisdom of the East to the West.

In the inner planes he became Master of the Council of the Royal Teton Retreat, which is where the Great White Brotherhood meets. In recent times, until he took over the second ray he supported one of Earth's twin planets, Metatron, which is more evolved than we are. Lord Lanto works with Archangel Jophiel to help people open the crown chakra through enlightenment.

Past incarnations of Lord Lanto

Lanto was a high priest in the temple of the Divine Mother in Lemuria.

He incarnated several times in China, always as a wise philosopher who spread great light. One of his incarnations was as the Duke of Chou where he taught Confucius, who subsequently ascended.

Chapter Twenty Seven

Ray 3 – Paul the Venetian

Ray 3 is a glorious sunshine yellow and is known as the ray of intelligence and creative activity. This ray is also associated with the pink of love.

If you work with the yellow aspect from your lower personality you may be too much in your head or absent minded, inflexible in your approach, inaccurate, proud or isolated. However, if your soul is filled with its beautiful light you radiate love, happiness, joy and you actively express your creativity through art, in a practical way. You will have a clear vision and will persevere with determination until it is fulfilled.

Your strength and tenacity, attention to detail and ability to imagine glorious concepts mean that you will push forward the divine plan for Earth. You will do something which will benefit humanity even after your death.

The negative personality influence of the pink aspect is needy, jealous or conditional love. When the pink shines through the soul, your unconditional love and warmth embraces the world with love.

Serapis Bey was the master of this ray. Now he has passed all the tests it offers and as an Initiate of it he has moved to become Chohan of the fourth ray.

Paul the Venetian

Paul the Venetian, who is also known as Master Paul, is the master or Chohan of this ray. He works closely with Master Rakoczy, who is now master of the eleventh ray and also with Archangel Zadkiel. They co-operate to develop your artistic and creative aspects as well as scientific and practical ideas. He teaches love in action and inspires people to perform loving deeds.

This wonderful yellow colour lifts people's spirits and sets their souls free, so that they can express their higher visions and he uses the beautiful pink of love to help musicians and artists and all creative endeavours.

It is Paul the Venetian who is introducing gentle high frequency pastel shades to Earth. All the shimmering silver or gold backed colours that are so popular have come from him. He influences gardeners to produce a huge variety of new colours in flowers and is opening our consciousness so that we can see a greater range of colour frequencies.

He has always been concerned with freedom and liberty. He was one of those who influenced the gift of the statue of liberty to New York.

You can access the energy of Paul the Venetian with Seraphiel in the Orb in picture (10).

Paul the Venetian's past incarnations

He was head of cultural affairs in Atlantis. Before that civilisation ended he took the Flame of Liberty from the Temple of the Sun to Peru. This was in order to prepare the land for Thoth, who led his tribe here at the end of Atlantis, to form the Inca civilisation. He incarnated in Egypt where he worked as a sacred architect. He was the painter Paulo Veronese, during the Renaissance, who expressed divine energy through colour and even then created new colours and painting techniques. He was also a priest in the Temple of the Sun in New York and still sends energy through the Statue of Liberty, which enables people to hold the vision of freedom.

Chapter Twenty Eight

Ray 4 – Serapis Bey

Ray 4 is a shimmering emerald green for this is the ray of harmony and balance. Those who are influenced by this ray at a personality level are trying to find this harmony and balance within themselves. So they often experience emotional highs and lows as they struggle with conflicting aspects of their personality. At lower levels they may manipulate, be lazy and lack self discipline.

When you merge this green into your soul, you will radiate harmony wherever you go. You will be a peacemaker, an artist or musician spreading beautiful energies to others. You will find inner serenity, self discipline, good judgement and confidence so that people will trust you.

Serapis Bey

Serapis Bey is the chohan or master of the fourth ray. He originated from Venus, the planet of the heart. He has an extraordinary and special role for he is the only master to work with the Seraphim to help them with their evolution.

The amethyst and violet rays are the rays of the Age of Aquarius. Serapis Bey is working with these as well as the green ray of balance and nature to bring forward a new way of thinking and learning for the New Age. He is also helping to establish more appropriate healing methods for people who are becoming more sensitive as their frequencies rise. This includes using sound waves, lasers, colour and non invasive techniques.

He is often called the Egyptian because his presence is felt strongly there. Also, after the fall of Atlantis, he worked with the angels to influence the building of the Pyramids, where his teachings are hidden at a fourth dimensional level. They will be accessed when people raise their consciousness sufficiently. Then we will have the possibility of co-operative world government for the highest good of all. He is the Keeper of the White Flame, which is the ascension flame. You can invoke it and step into its energy for purification and raising of your light levels.

Serapis Bey has an ascension chamber in the etheric above Luxor, which you can visit in your sleep time, if you prepare yourself and ask to go there.

Serapis Bey's past incarnations

Serapis Bey was a great priest Avatar in the Ascension Temple in Atlantis. He was also Solomon, Zoroaster and Akhenaton IV, the Pharoah who protected and reorganised the Great White Brotherhood during his reign and brought back an understanding of one God. He was also the Pharaoh Amenophis.

Chapter Twenty Nine

Ray 5 – Hilarion

This is the orange ray of science, technology, wisdom, truth and knowledge, which covers occult as well as practical science. If your personality is suffused in this ray you may be nit picking, narrow minded or pedantic. However if your soul is working with this ray you will stand for justice and fairness, honour and truth. You will want to probe deeply for answers and bring them forward in a way to help humanity as a whole.

Master Hilarion

Hilarion remains for the time being as Chohan of the fifth ray, which is orange, though he also works with the mind colour, yellow, in order to stimulate an understanding of practical as well as esoteric science and technology for the New Age. He directs energy to help those who are ready to become higher channels and clairvoyants. It is Hilarion who visits scientists, healers or technologists to drop the seeds of new ideas into their consciousness. For example, he worked with the angels and technologists to bring about digital cameras which vibrated at the same frequency as Orbs.

We were sent a stunning Orb, which unfortunately did not reproduce well enough to put in this book, of Hilarion being brought by an archangel to watch a spider weaving its web. He came to learn about sacred geometry from the spider. The web is a simple concept, intricately designed. Kumeka told us that humans would see the problems of constructing something like this against gravity. They would tend to focus on the difficulties. The spider, however, simply holds the vision of the final outcome and so it is accomplished. It is a reminder to envision the end result with faith and miracles occur.

Hilarion's previous incarnations

Hilarion worked in Atlantis in the Temple of Truth. In Greece he established the Oracle of Delphi. He was Paul the Apostle and was also Saint Hilarion a hermit and healer who performed miracles.

He collaborates closely with Master Marko who represents the highest Galactic confederation of our solar system, the capital of which is on Saturn. He is also the negotiator for Earth on the Council of Saturn to help us remain connected to our Spiritual journey.

Chapter Thirty

Ray 6 – Mary Magdelene

T his is the indigo ray of idealism and devotion, which was influential for 2,000 years during the Piscean Age, a time when people expected to follow gurus or saints. With the arrival of the Aquarian Age the emphasis of this ray has changed. Now, if your lower personality is dominated by this ray you might be bigoted, narrow, over idealistic or dogmatically religious.

However if your soul is bathed in this ray, you have incarnated to transform dogmatic thinking in religion into independent thinking with unconditional love, so that people can open their hearts and minds to God. You will try to unite different sects and religions.

Mary Magdelene

Mary Magdelene has become the master of the sixth ray to bring in the influence of the divine feminine into religion. She is also bringing in new healing methods. Like Jesus she originated from Venus.

Mary Magdelene's previous incarnations

During her incarnation with Jesus, she was his spiritual partner and a master in her own right. They walked the chakra trail together, the path of sacred cathedrals originally built by the Knights Templar. Her retreat is in the etheric above Rosslyn Chapel, Scotland, which represents the crown chakra on this sacred journey.

She was a healer in Lemuria, a High Priestess in a Mayan healing temple and also an Aztec healer.

Archangels Michael, Gabriel, Uriel and Zadkiel accompanying Mary Magdelene

When you look at Orb (34) you receive the ability to open your right brain to understand and express wisdom, unconditional love and peace and spread it to the world.

In Orb (34) Archangel Michael is protecting Mary Magdelene. Archangel Zadkiel is clearing the path for her arrival by transmuting the energy through which the Orb travels. Archangel Gabriel is purifying the people who are to receive her message, so that they will be ready to accept it. Archangel Uriel is radiating the divine masculine energy to the world, while Mary Magdelene is bringing in the divine feminine, which is about healing with love and compassion. She is offering keys to open the right brain to enable you to access the ancient wisdom from Atlantis which she is carrying. This is being brought forward in the New Age as non invasive healing techniques. She is taking blinkers off people about old rigid ways of doing things and is also helping them to communicate lovingly with each other and to make their own communication with Source.

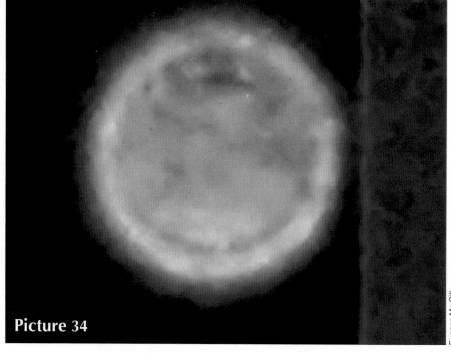

Picture 34

Eugene Mc Gill

Chapter Thirty One

Ray 7 – Lady Nada

Ray 7 is the violet ray of ritual, ceremony and magic, which is coming in strongly now that the Aquarian Age has fully arrived. Violet is the colour of transmutation and much is currently being released and purified within individuals and the world. If your personality is dominated by this ray you will be superstitious, bigoted, easily influenced or narrow. However if your soul is working with this light you will love ceremonies and rituals which bring people together and raise high energy. You will practise self discipline and be ordered. You may be a New Age healer or leader, creative or work to bring about unity and higher understandings.

Lady Nada

Lady Nada, the twin flame of Jesus, has taken over the seventh ray, which is the most influential ray for the Age of Aquarius. She is a member of the Karmic Board and has always defended the oppressed and acted for justice. She is bringing back ancient healing methods, helping with the development of intuition, telepathy and wisdom.

Lady Nada's past lives

In Atlantis Lady Nada was a priestess in the Temple of Love. She was Elizabeth, mother of John the Baptist. She also promoted Islamic art at the time of the Prophet Mohammed.

Chapter Thirty Two

Ray 8 – Lord Kumeka

The Higher Rays

These new rays are soul rays and do not attach to the personality. If you are influenced by one of these, you will respond to the highest potential of the colour being sent to you

Ray 8 is the topaz blue ray of deep transmutation, purification, enlightenment and communication. When you work with this ray you have a desire to heal and release your past and you will want to extend this to the healing and releasing of others. You are on a quest for enlightenment.

This ray will enable people to clean up their act so that they move towards the divine. It also clears and prepares places for the changes ahead.

Master Kumeka

Kumeka is the Lord of Light who is the master of the eighth ray. He came from a different universe. He is my guide and worked with and through me for many years before I came onto a conscious spiritual path or was aware of the spiritual world. He is instrumental in enlightening the world and bringing it to ascension and is one of the busiest of all the masters.

Chapter Thirty Three

Ray 9 – Lord Voosloo

Ray 9 started to shine once more onto this planet in 2001. The yellow ray of harmony is working to balance the mind and spirit of humanity. The aim is to bring spirit and intellect into harmony, without the negative ego coming into play.

Master Voosloo

Voosloo is the Master of the ninth ray. He was the greatest and purest of all the High Priests of Atlantis and understands exactly what went wrong at that time. He has undertaken to bring back balance to the world, ensuring that we do not make the same mistakes as we did before.

Voosloo's previous incarnation

He was a wise one of Mu, the civilisation before Lemuria.

Archangels Gabriel and Uriel
with the Power Wywyvsil and Master Voosloo

When you look at Orb (35) you receive a sense of the vastness of the universe and can help humanity ascend.

Archangel Gabriel is bringing Lord Voosloo to ensure that as you look at the Orb in picture (35) your intentions are pure and you become clear about them. Archangel Uriel gives you the strength to do what you need to do on your ascension pathway.

Wywyvsil is a power, one of the higher ranking levels of the angelic hierarchy and is a Lord of Karma. He has come with this Orb to protect Voosloo and to assess the changes made by humanity. He is then taking the information back to teach about it in his inner planes schools, where he is teaching some of the new ascended masters.

One of these is Kathy Crosswell's brother, George, who ascended when he passed over in 2007, and can be seen in Orb (42). Through this Orb Wywyvsil is issuing an invitation to you to visit his schools in the inner planes, during your sleep, for higher cosmic teachings. In addition as you look at this Orb he helps you to find your soul's purpose, not just for this life but in the universe.

Lord Voosloo is helping your ascension process. He was the greatest and highest frequency High Priest/Priestess of Atlantis that ever incarnated in that role. He was so evolved that he had totally balanced his masculine and feminine aspects and was androgynous. He originates from another Universe and when he comes to Earth, he steps his frequency down through Neptune. He has returned to work with Earth again as Chohan or Master of the ninth ray to bring balance back to humanity and is very much connected with the ascension of our planet.

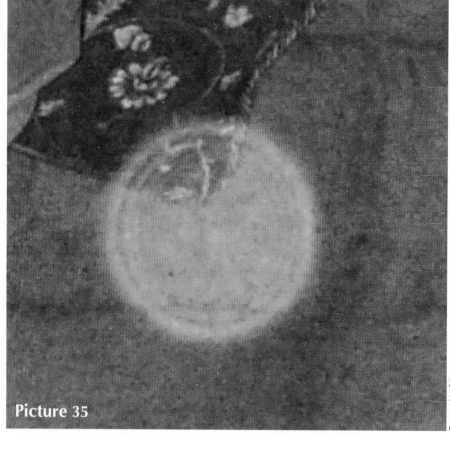

Picture 35

Eugene Mc Gill

Chapter Thirty Four

Ray 10 – Lord Gautama

Ray 10 came back to the planet at the end of 2001. It is citrine and carries Buddha energy. When this ray influences you it enables you to find your true life purpose and to action it in a grounded and practical way.

Lord Gautama

Lord Gautama is the Master of this ray. He was Prince Siddartha Gautama, the son of an Indian Emperor, at which time he incarnated without karma. He renounced his fortune, left his wife and child and became an ascetic. After years of meditation he gained enlightenment and was transfigured, becoming the Buddha at the full moon in 544BC, now known as the Wesak moon. Then in a great act of renunciation he brought his vibration down again so that he could be fully in a physical body and serve humanity again. He was the first person from this planet to hold the position of Buddha, the embodiment of wisdom.

Lord Gautama's previous incarnations

He was incarnated in Lemuria, was Hermes of ancient Egypt, Orpheus of Greece and Thoth in Atlantis.

Chapter Thirty Five

Ray 11 – Rakoczy

Ray 11 is the ray of clarity, mysticism and healing, which came back to the planet at the end of 2001 and the colour is bright, vibrant, deep emerald.

Rakoczy

Rakoczy, an incarnation of St. Germain, is the Master of this ray. He is working to bring peace, understanding and enlightenment to world leaders to bring about an improvement in international affairs. He is doing the same with religions to eliminate entrenched ideas. Another of his tasks is to help the human body to make changes so that it can cope with increasing pollution of every kind and then accept the higher energies now available.

Master Rakoczy's past incarnations

Rakoczy was one of the incarnations of St. Germain, who used to be Lord of Civilization. Other incarnations were Samuel the prophet, Lao-Tze, the Chinese philosopher, Joseph of Nazareth, St Alban, Proclus the Greek philosopher, Merlin the Magician, Christopher Columbus and Francis Bacon. As Christian Rosenkreutz he founded the order of the Rosy Cross, which later became the Rosicrucians.

Archangels Michael, Uriel, Gabriel and Raphael, a unicorn and Master Rakoczy

When you look at Orb (36) you will receive the courage to go out and make a difference.

Orb (36) contains Archangels Michael, Uriel, Gabriel and Raphael as well as unicorn energy and Rakoczy. Archangel Michael is protecting the Master Rakoczy. Archangel Uriel is giving people who work with this Orb confidence and a sense of self worth, so they can find the courage to take action towards their vision.

Archangel Gabriel is bringing you clarity so that you can receive the healing which Archangel Raphael is sending out. The unicorn is bringing enlightenment while Rakoczy is helping you to activate your vision for the world.

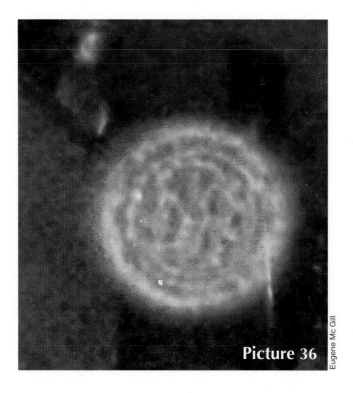

Picture 36

Eugene Mc Gill

Chapter Thirty Six
Ray 12 – Quan Yin

Ray 12 entered the planet in 2003. It is the ray of unconditional love, the colour being bright cerise pink.

Quan Yin

Quan Yin is the Master of this ray, which carries the divine feminine energy. She sits on the board of the Lords of Karma. Her task is to bring forward the divine feminine wisdom, healing and compassion within men and women. To do this she is helping women to re-empower themselves.

Quan Yin's past incarnations

She held the energy of the temple of love in Lemuria but did not incarnate as the people then were not fully physicalised. She had many lifetimes in China and was considered a Goddess.

Archangels Michael, Raphael and Zadkiel with Quan Yin

When you look at Orb (37) you receive help to use your masculine energy positively and move on to your ascension pathway.

Orb (37) contains Archangels Michael, Raphael and Zadkiel bringing the divine feminine and the divine masculine aspects of Quan Yin. The divine masculine has never incarnated but overlights her and is holding her light on Earth. He protects those who work with her and have her energy, so that they are not influenced by negative aspects of other people's masculine energy.

Many people have too much masculine energy and this is holding them back on their ascension journey. This Orb helps to soothe and heal them.

In picture (37) Archangel Michael is protecting Quan Yin. Archangel Zadkiel is transmuting any negative energy which they go through on their journey as they search for their target. Archangel Raphael and Quan Yin are radiating healing.

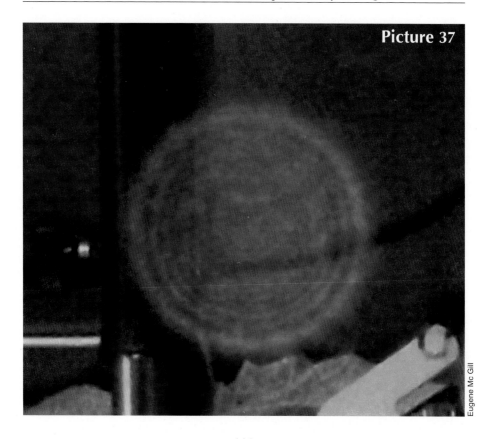

Eugene Mc Gill

***

Masculine energy

In olden times when males had to hunt for food and protect their wives and families, they were strong, protective and focussed on catching their game no matter what. They needed testosterone to fuel this primary survival task. The masculine energy is connected with the logical, ordered left brain, which results in short term outcomes, accentuates differences and creates decisions which are made from the mind not the heart. This means things are thought through but not felt through and can lead to a lack of harmony and trust, even aggression or in extreme cases, heartless cruelty.

The Piscean Age was dominated by the masculine energy, so that structure and order, rules and regulations were imposed without common sense. Religious dogma was inevitable. This is beginning to change as we move into the Aquarian age but the masculine still prevails and, in those communities without heart, people do not feel a sense of security. This means that they strive for material possessions as a substitute and naturally the economy becomes an important focus.

Left brain societies and individuals do thrust forward with technology, science and inventions but this is usually at the expense of caring and nature. When you have a wholly masculine ordered society individuals and groups often feel empty, lost, frightened, fractured or, if they dare, rebellious.

In societies with a focus on the development of the right brain, caring, empathy, trust, nurturing and inclusivity is encouraged and valued. This leads to relaxation, peace and contentment but sometimes lack of decision-making powers or financial acumen.

Feminine energy

Feminine energy is open hearted, nurturing, inclusive, co-operative, peaceful and happy. The right brain is original, creative, imaginative, artistic and musical. It sees an overall, helicopter view, values good communications and seeks solutions that will benefit everyone. Those people and societies who are feminine orientated foster the arts and support the spiritual and mystical. It is through the right brain that you connect with the spiritual world and ascension.

The out of balance feminine energy is ungrounded, so the economy stagnates and there is a lack of scientific or technological development.

Balanced masculine and feminine

This is the ideal as in a perfect old fashioned marriage. The female is wise and nurturing, keeps communication alive and brings through original creations and spiritual connections. The male supports her original ideas, thinks things through logically and puts energy into making them manifest. He also follows her spiritual lead and protects her in every way. She tempers his rules and tendency to control with her wisdom.

The individual who has balanced their own masculine and feminine is ready for the ascension journey.

Chapter Thirty Seven

Babaji

Orb picture (38) was taken after a Dru yoga class led by Jenny. The Orb is of Archangel Christiel bringing Babaji, the great yogi known as the deathless avatar, to watch the meditation at the end of the session. We were told that, because Jenny was about to attend a week long silent retreat, he had come to observe her meditation teaching as help could be offered while she was on retreat. Three weeks later, after her return, Babaji returned once more to assess her progress, brought by her guardian angel with an angel of love. If only we knew how our spiritual work was being monitored.

Jenny told me of an experience that happened a few years ago when she and a friend were returning from a pilgrimage in the Himalayas, having visited the source of the Ganges and other holy sites. At Rudraprayag, the holy confluence of Alaknanda and Mandakini rivers, which eventually becomes the Ganges, they were approached by an old man who led them down to the confluence of the rivers. Here they stood in the swirling, icy waters while he chanted for a long time and finally a blessing was given.

Returning up the steps they became aware of a young man in a loin cloth beckoning them into a cave. He was very beautiful and reminded them of pictures they'd seen of Babaji. They noticed he had a small picture of Babaji on a rock shelf at the back of the cave and he said he was a devotee. They were invited to eat with him (though there didn't appear to be any food in the cave!) but unfortunately, after a short time sitting with him, had to return up the hill in time to catch the bus.

I wondered if it could have been Babaji, so we asked Kumeka who told us that Babaji could divide into many aspects of himself, just like archangels. He said that the young man was a devotee of Babaji and the great avatar had been overlighting him at the time. The meeting with Jenny and her friend had been orchestrated by spirit and the cleansing in the river was an important part of the preparation.

Babaji

Much is written about this extraordinary yogi, who is a Mahavatar. Mahavatar means great avatar, while Babaji means revered father and he carries Source energy in a physical body. He has lived on Earth for thousands of years, appearing at times throughout history when the world most needs his light. But he has always watched over the progress of humankind.

Babaji is known as the deathless avatar because he took the decision to remain on Earth in service to humanity. He shows himself as an eternally young man. He has yogic powers or Siddhas and uses these for the healing or enhancement of humanity. He has been witnessed on occasions to sit on water, to materialise and dematerialise himself as well as to heal the sick.

There are many recorded meetings with Babaji between 1861 and 1935 when he initiated those who were ready into Krija Yoga. This is a system of yoga which breaks down the old resistances to God and accelerates ascension. He was in constant communion with Christ to inspire the world and spread self liberation through yoga in the West as well as in the East. He teaches about the saving grace of Truth, Simplicity and Love and advocates the chanting of Om Namah Shivaya to lead you to God.

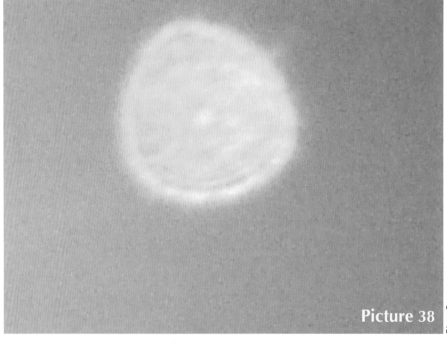

Picture 38

Diana Cooper

Babaji appeared in 1970 in the historic holy cave situated at the foot of Kumaon Mount Adi Kailash. He has also shown himself in Nepal and other places. Paramahansa Yogananda in his book *Autobiography of a Yogi* describes his meeting with him.

Archangel Christiel with Babaji

When you look at Orb (38) you will receive a knowing that your journey is constantly watched over and assessed.

Throughout your life there is regular feedback by your guides, angels and archangels to the archangel who is overseeing your life. This Orb reminds you that you are never forgotten and when you are ready for new spiritual teaching it will be brought to you.

Chapter Thirty Eight

St. Theresa of Avila, St. Clare

St Theresa has had many lifetimes on Earth. There are many working under her influence while still in a body and she leads a team of lightworkers in the inner planes. She is spreading an understanding of Oneness with Source within religions instead of the old forms of dogma and structure.

Previous incarnations of St Theresa

During each of her eleven incarnations St. Theresa was a nun and many of these religious experiences were in Italy. They prepared her for her role as one of the higher hierarchy taking the consciousness of the world beyond religious structure into unconditional love.

St. Clare

St. Clare originates from Venus, the planet of the heart. In her best known lifetime she was influenced by St Francis to renounce her riches and found the Poor Clares, an order of nuns who lived in poverty and devoted their lives to service to God.

She is less well known for her life as Pontius Pilate's wife where she affected a great many people, for her soul energy was about service. Again she was a very determined and strong personality, motivated by goodness, kindness and gentleness. She always saw the divine in others and tried to reason with her husband and soften his approach. Even though she did not succeed she did her best and knew she was not responsible for his decisions or actions.

As an ascended master of the higher hierarchy she holds the Christ light up to people and helps them to see the divine in themselves and others. She is influencing individuals to act with goodness but not to take responsibility for the behaviour of others. So she helps people to cut the ties to relationships that do not serve the greater good. This particularly applies to dead or abusive relationships between partners, business associates or even family members.

Archangels Chamuel, Metatron and Zadkiel with St. Clare

When you look at Orb (39) you will receive unconditional love and humility about your role in the divine plan.

Archangel Chamuel is radiating love to open your heart chakra, while Archangel Zadkiel is protecting St. Clare by transmuting negative energy through which the Orb has to travel. Archangel Metatron is preparing your Stellar Gateway to receive unconditional love and humbleness about your part in the ascension of the planet

Picture 39

Eugene Mc Gill

***

Chapter Thirty Nine

Jesus, Kuthumi, St. Germain, Dwjhal Kuhl

Jesus

2000 years ago the spiritual hierarchy realised that something must be done to raise the energy on Earth. They decided that the Christ light, which is a cosmic force of pure unconditional love, was to be brought down to the people. It was to be carried by one man. It had to be a male because females at this time were considered inferior and were treated as chattels. Only a male would be respected.

Clearly a man who could carry the Christ energy must be a very pure and evolved soul. He must also be born of a chaste and holy, mother and to a wise and devoted father. The grandparents too were important as was the whole family.

The Essene brotherhood had a great secret temple at Heliopolis in Egypt where the highest ceremonies were held. It was known as the temple of Helios or to some, the Temple of the Sun. Joachim, was the High Priest in this temple and Anna was his wife. They taught the Great White Brotherhood teachings. When Mary was born to them they agreed the baby should become a dove of the temple, a vestal virgin, who would be educated and spiritually trained to a very high degree by the priests. I write about Mother Mary in Chapter 16 and tell more of her story in *The Web of Light*.

Joseph was a carpenter, really a master builder, and a devout Essene and Member of the Great White Brotherhood.

Jesus originates from Venus and was born to them in an Essene grotto or hospice, in the spring when the lambs were in the fields. He was a divine conception, as have been many Avatars including Krishna, Buddha, Lao-Tsze of China, Horus, Ra of Egypt, Zoroaster of Persia, Quetzalcoatl of Mexico, Plato and Pythagoras. His birth was attended by three wise men, Balthazar (Lord Kuthumi), Melchior (El Morya) and Caspar (Dwjhal Kuhl).

It was not until the fifth century, after years of dispute, that his official birthday was decreed by the Holy Fathers as the 25th December, which is an annual time of mystic significance. A cosmic change occurs at midnight of 24th December, bringing in a rush of new divine energy, which is why that date was already celebrated as a religious festival in India, China, Egypt, Mexico and others. Because of this energy many of the great masters chose to celebrate their birthdays on this date.

He was named Jeshua Ben Joseph and was registered as Joseph when he entered school at Mount Carmel, the great mystery school for the Great White Brotherhood.

'Joseph' learnt Aramaic, Hebrew and the Greek languages, astrology, astronomy, the natural laws of the universe and studied the major religions. He was also taught the sacred mysteries, to practise mind control and underwent very challenging initiations.

In order to become a pure instrument for the cosmic Christ his education was carefully planned. At the age of thirteen He left Mount Carmel and then travelled with the Magi to Jagannath, now known as Puri, India, to study pure Buddhism.

In Benares He studied ethics, natural law and languages and was also taught the Hindu principles of healing. Then back in the monastery of Jagannath, He studied documents sent from Tibet by Mengtse, the Buddhist sage. Then he travelled to Persia, the Euphrates, Babylon, Greece, under Apollonius, and on to Alexandria. Finally at the Supreme Temple at Heliopolis He prepared for initiation into the Higher Grades of the Great White Brotherhood. He became a High Priest in the Order of Melchizidek.

He attained the name of Jesus the Christ at a great secret ceremony within the Great Pyramid. Then he was overlit by Lord Meitreya, the head of the spiritual hierarchy. His purpose was to carry the Christ consciousness and touch the hearts of the masses.

Why was Jesus crucified?

The Great Pyramid is a huge antennae out into the universe as well as a cosmic computer. It is also a portal to four planets, which are helping with the ascension of Earth. These four planets hold our energy, send healing and light and help keep us on our path. They are Orion, Sirius, the Pleiades and Neptune. Until recently Neptune was known as the hidden planet because its purpose was not realised. These four planets were intimately connected with holding Earth steady while the Christ energy entered into this plane of existence.

There was a master who was entrusted with holding all this energy together so that Jesus could fulfil his purpose. Unfortunately she underestimated the power of the anger of those whose lifestyle was being endangered. Huge waves of dark energy were released and she could not hold it back. It threatened to implode the whole plan as well as the planet so to prevent dire consequences she cut away

Neptune from the other three planets, which allowed the dark energy to escape into the universe. See the Metatron cube, picture (29) on page 93.

The consequence was that Earth spun downward into lower consciousness for two thousand years. Now it is changing and rising in frequency again, so when we reconnect Neptune to the Pyramid once more, the planet can ascend.

What you can do to help reconnect Neptune?

Just looking at the sacred geometry of the planetary Metatron Cube (picture 29) which we present in this book can help reconnect the links with Neptune and bring everything back into alignment. Your visualisation of the wholeness of the divine plan as represented in the planetary Cube makes you into a divine Creator.

You can also pray for the reconnection of the energetic lines and for the soul of the master who could not hold the energy at the time of Christ. Now back in incarnation her soul feels guilty though no blame is attached to her.

Past incarnations of Jesus

He was Jeshua, Joseph of Egypt, Adam, Elijah and ascended many times from Earth.

Did Krishna carry the Christ light?

Yes.

Lord Kuthumi

Lord Kuthumi was the Chohan of the Second Ray, the teaching ray and he has been promoted to World Teacher. He is the Hierophant of the brotherhood of the Golden Robe; Great Ones who take on the pain of the world. If you find that you are very sensitive and take other people's emotional and physical pain through you, you may belong to this brotherhood.

In the etheric above Kashmir, Lord Kuthumi has an enormous ashram for students, helping them and the planet to evolve on the ascension path. He also has a Light Chamber in the etheric above Machu Picchu to help our understanding. However his main retreat is in the etheric in Agra, India above the Taj Mahal.

Like Jesus the Christ, Kuthumi's teacher was Lord Meitreya, who is head of the Spiritual Hierarchy. With El Morya and Djwhal Khul, he also brought Theosophy to the world.

Past incarnations

He was Pythagoras, Balthazar, one of the Three Wise Men, John the Beloved, Shah Jahan who built the Taj Mahal and St. Francis of Assisi.

Picture 40

Mandy Whalley

Archangel Faith, Lord Kuthumi and Master Imor

When you look at picture (40) you receive a total trust in divine connections.

In Picture (40) the three shooting Orbs are: On the left, Archangel Faith, twin flame of Gabriel. She is helping people to hold faith that they are on the right path. In the middle is Lord Kuthumi, the World Teacher, who is opening people up to receive the spiritual teachings of the universe. On the right, the yellow Orb is Master Imor, who is working with Archangel Jophiel to bring energy from Source into you. He helps people to access their higher wisdom.

Looking at these great beings helps attune you to higher frequencies.

***

St. Germain

St. Germain used to be the master of the seventh ray, the violet ray and while he was its chohan, in 1987, he brought back for humanity the Violet Flame of Transmutation. This started the twenty five year period of purification leading to 2012. He was the Lord of Civilization but has been promoted again within the spiritual hierarchy of Earth. He is now one of those in charge of overseeing the ascension of this planet. He is working with the Lords of Karma and bringing back a sense of spiritual values to people on Earth. His task is to establish balance once more and he is known as the Keeper of the Golden Scales.

Previous incarnations

Samuel the prophet, Joseph of Nazareth, Rakoczy, St Alban, Proclus the Greek philosopher, Merlin the Magician, Christopher Columbus, Francis Bacon. As Christian Rosenkreutz he founded the order of the Rosy Cross, which later became the Rosicrucians.

Dwjhal Kuhl

Dwjhal Khul has always worked with Lord Kuthumi and now teaches many of his students as well as those of the other masters. Like Lord Kuthumi he belongs to the Brotherhood of the Golden Robe. He is often referred to as The Tibetan because he and Vuywamus started the Tibetan Foundation, working with Alice Bailey to bring through esoteric information. At the time this was a breath taking breakthrough to raise the frequency of those who were ready. Vuywamus originated from Venus and is the higher self of Sanat Kumara, who is the Planetary Logos, the greatest of the Avatars. He has now returned to Venus to undertake new work though he still connects with his students on Earth.

Previous incarnations – He was one of the three wise men and Johan Sebastian Bach.

Chapter Forty

Lord Meitreya and Lord Melchizedek

Lord Meitreya

Lord Meitreya is the great master who overlit Jesus from birth and on the cross. He draws love directly from Source and steps it down through the cosmic heart, which is a pool of pure white universal energy to spread to humanity. He works with all the archangels especially Archangel Chamuel of the heart chakra to radiate the heart light.

He is waking up those who contracted to take the ascension pathway in this lifetime as well as those who are ready even though it was not part of their birth plan. (They have worked hard to clear their karma). When you are ready your light switches on and he is looking for you and finds you. Then he holds you in his light. Imagine he is pouring down a ray of sunshine over you but sending only the frequency that you can cope with.

He is instrumental in helping you connect with your higher guides. Then he keeps his connection with you through them.

Lord Melchizedek

Lord Melchizedek, known as the Eternal Lord of Light is head of the vast universal brotherhood known as the Melchizedek priesthood and receives directly the teachings of God. He is not one individual but a group energy, rather like the Mahatma, to which many beings contribute their light to enhance the purpose.

Only a few incarnate and those who receive spiritual illumination within the order, like Abraham, Moses, Elijah, David and Jesus become High Priests.

A Melchizedek will be sent to help wherever there is an emergency, crisis or need for their light in the universe. Jesus was one such example, who came to Earth to assist the Creator's plan for love on this planet.

Chapter Forty One

Commander Ashtar

We were sent a photograph taken at Machu Picchu of an Orb carrying Commandar Ashtar and Thoth, who were bringing their energy to you. We would love to have had permission to use the photograph, for the Orb contained an invitation to go out into the galaxies of this universe, and the angels asked us to write about it and the reason it had allowed itself to be photographed at Machu Picchu.

Machu Picchu

Machu Picchu in Peru, is one of the four inter-dimensional portals on the planet. The first of my trilogy of novels is *The Silent Stones*, part of which is set in Machu Picchu. In that book I offer a great deal of fascinating esoteric information about this extraordinary place.

The portal of Machu Picchu needs to be used and kept pure by spiritual people in order to raise its energy. Commander Ashtar's space ships come through here. They do not need to enter through this place, but when they do people can often see them with their naked eyes and photograph them. The space ships bring in what we call aliens, but they are really friendly and highly evolved beings from other planets, to connect with humans. (We do not say that all extra terrestrials are friendly but those transported by Commandar Ashtar's command are). They are invisible to most people but an unconscious connection is made to remind us that there is a whole world out there.

Commander Ashtar

Commander Ashtar belongs to the Hierarchy of the Great Central Sun. He is the commander of the intergalactic fleet, which is a vast fleet of spaceships stationed near Earth which patrol this universe. He is a very high frequency master who is working for the greater good of our planet and particularly to wake people up to their spiritual potential. He also protects us and the planet. Much light is being beamed from his space ships to humans and he is also issuing invitations to those who go to Machu Picchu to travel on his spaceships and journey intergalactically in this universe.

When you visit Machu Picchu you are subconsciously reminded that you can ascend. Commander Ashtar is working with the unicorns and when he comes here many of them accompany him to bring enlightenment and ascension. They shine their light into this ascension city.

Thoth

Thoth was one of the original twelve High Priests and Priestesses of Atlantis at the commencement of the Golden Age. He returned to those islands when the experiment of Atlantis was terminated to lead his tribe into a specially prepared place. Elsewhere in this book I describe how Paul took the Flame of Liberty from the Temple of the Sun in Atlantis to Peru in order to prepare the land for Thoth's people. Thoth then established the Inca civilization. It was the Inca wise ones who built the sacred portal of Machu Picchu, hidden in the mountains. It could only be entered via a tortuous climb, during which they had to undertake a number of purification rituals.

As a High Priest in Atlantis, Thoth had access to the Intergalactic Council and from them he channelled the spiritual laws for Earth. Using his enormous power he used the metals from the planet to set the ley lines and these were used to enable people of that time to fly. Thoth guards the portal of Machu Picchu.

He organises the whole scheme of crop circles on Earth and beyond. It is he who allows through the angels of communication and their teams of helpers, who make the crop circles and arranges for them to be placed where their messages are most needed. Many are placed near Avebury in the West Country of the U.K. because this area is preparing for spiritual work ahead. They are also being placed in China to persuade people to open their right brain as they explore the rationally inexplicable.

As soon as we realised that the Machu Picchu invitation could not be shown Kathy took a picture of her son Harry. On him was an Orb which was angels with a master. I laughed because I knew immediately it was Commander Ashtar and Kathy said that he was passionately interested in space and interstellar connections.

**Angels of Archangels Gabriel and Michael
with Commander Ashtar**

When you look at picture (41) you receive an invitation to travel intergalactically with Commander Ashtar.

Chapter Forty Two

The Newly Ascended Masters

George

Kathy's brother George died in 2007 aged only fifty-five years old but he was a very special man and he ascended as he passed over. He has also ascended from other lifetimes. Kathy told me he has been a pilot in several lifetimes and always died when his vehicle crashed. In the distant past he piloted a space ship and much more recently an aeroplane in World War 2, when he flew many successful missions until his plane crashed on landing. Clearly he re-incarnated very quickly in order to experience the current conditions of Earth and in this last life he enjoyed science and technology. On the other side he is now teaching the spirits of children who have passed and also the spirits of those who are still alive who travel while they are asleep, about higher scientific principles. He is working with Pythagoras teaching sacred geometry and with Metatron and Hilarion. He is also helping to bring forward the Orbs. Kathy says he will love doing this.

Picture 42a

Diana Cooper

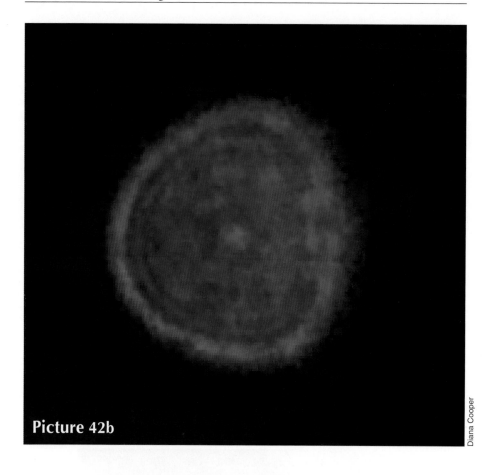

Picture 42b

Diana Cooper

Archangel Christiel and Master George

When you look at Orb (42) you receive a connection with the scientific masters in alignment with the divine plan.

I took the picture of Orb (42a/b) at Kathy's house after we had been working together to bring forward information for this book. Really I was just snapping her animals to see if there were any Orbs and was delighted when there were several. But her Rottweiler Jake, who was lying on his back on the floor, suddenly turned his head away as I took the picture. As you can see he was happily looking at the Orb which has come into the room. It is Archangel Christiel bringing her brother, Master George.

***

Eugene McGill's mother

When Eugene sent us the beautiful Orbs that we have published in this book, he said that he had taken them when his mother passed away in their home. He added that when his mother was buried on the winter solstice, 21st December 2007 there was a sea of souls outside their house.

We were told by Archangel Michael that the archangels brought the great ascended masters to collect her because she was ascending. What a wonderful reception to Heaven.

His mother is now teaching children who have passed over about spirituality and giving them cosmic information so that they can have an expanded view. She is also teaching the spirits of some children in their sleep.

I spoke to Eugene on the phone about his mother and he talked of her with great love. He described her as a star, a real good woman. She was a typical devoted mother of six and the grandmother of six much adored grandchildren. Eugene described her as a warm, caring person who had time for everyone and was always very positive. She loved landscape painting and gardening but was very modest about her talents.

He said there was an overwhelming sense of love in their home at the funeral. Someone even came up to him and said, 'I'm sorry for your loss but I've heard she was beautiful.' He also added that she looked so young, everyone remarked on it, and I am sure this must have been the light shining through her.

I loved his description of someone who lived an ordinary family life with such love, integrity and caring that she ascended.

Agatha's father's ascension

Agatha was holding her father's hand when he passed. She felt the most wonderful peace and joy filling her as he left his body, such as she has never experienced before or since. Later she was told she had received the Consolatum as he ascended. We learnt that the Consolatum is a gift from the angels as he passed because she was an instrument in helping him to ascend. When you help someone ascend you also receive the energy.

Chapter Forty Three

The Masters of Orion

O rion is one of the four planets very connected with the healing and ascension of Earth. It is known as the planet of Wisdom and Enlightenment because the beings from there have much higher degrees of cosmic understanding than we do. The others are the Pleiades, Sirius and Neptune.

I had a most extraordinary experience one day when I was standing by my open back door taking pictures of the garden. As I took the photograph, the Orb in picture (43) loomed so large on the screen, right in front of me, that I jumped back in shock. Later we learnt that the Orb was a unicorn carrying two Masters of Orion, who wanted to enter my consciousness to expand it. Unfortunately, my sudden movement backwards meant that they could not access my energy fields but Kumeka assured me that they would return. I was intrigued, so started to ask questions and this is what we were told.

Orion is ruled by the seven Masters of Orion, who shine seven rays onto Earth, each containing a different aspect of wisdom.

1. The ability to still the mind so that it is receptive when you listen.
2. The ability to feel the divine truth.
3. The ability to understand the divine truth at a deep level.
4. The ability to act on it.
5. The ability to teach it to others so they get it at a deep level.
6. The ability to feel who you are.
7. The ability to merge with God.

The great Masters of Orion were apparently bringing me rays 6 and 7.

When you look at Orb (43) you will want to know more and this will open up contacts to people who can help you.

A Unicorn bringing two Masters of Orion

When you look at Orb (43) you will receive an expansion of the mind to higher truths.

Picture 43

Chapter Forty Four

The Etheric Retreats of the Masters

Just as there are special places where you feel comfortable on Earth, the masters create retreats in the etheric of a location where they felt particularly at home. You can visit these places in meditation or during sleep, so that you may absorb the energy of the master or even receive their teachings or healing. In some cases the retreat is above the area, in others right in the middle of it. The clarity of your intention to visit is the one important factor that will take you there and the other is your ability to reach the vibration of that retreat.

Some people find it very beneficial to go to the physical location of the retreat, where they can pick up the light of the master more easily.

Titles of Ascended Masters

Most but not all ascended masters can be called by the title Master, whichever gender they are. It depends on their level of light. Those who are more evolved become Lords of Light and can be entitled Lord or Lady. Those who are saints I have referred to as St, for example St. Clare, though they are also Lords of Light. Melchizedek is a Lord of Light. However many energies come into him and when he becomes that group energy his frequency is higher than that of a Lord.

Lord El Morya and Master Abraham	They both have retreats in Calcutta, India and in Kashmir.
Lord Lanto	Deep in the forests of central China. He can also be accessed sometimes at the Royal Teton Retreat in the Teton Mountains in Wyoming.
Lord Paul the Venetian	The Chateau de Liberte, the Castle of Freedom, in the south of France.
Lord Serapis Bey	Above Luxor, Egypt.

Lord Hilarion	Hilarion comes from Saturn and steps his energy down through The Temple of Truth over Crete in Greece, where he has established his etheric retreat.
Lady Mary Magdelene	Above Rosslyn Chapel, Scotland.
Lady Nada	Over Saudi Arabia or Tibet.
Lord Kumeka	Above Caracas, Venezuela, South America. He also comes in through Knowle Church in Dorset, England.
*Lord Voosloo	Stonehenge, England.
Lord Gautama	The source of the Yangtze River.
Lord Rakoczy	The Kremlin. See Orb in picture (36)
Lady Quan Yin	The Silk Road, China.
Lord Babaji	The Himalayas.
St. Clare	Rome.
St Catherine	Sienna, Italy.
St. Theresa	Avila, Italy.
Lord Dwjhal Kuhl	Mumbai, India
Lord St. Germain	Koln (Cologne) Germany.
Lord Kuthumi	Agra, India.
Lord Jesus	Mount Olive, Israel (now very specifically working through an individual, who is a New Age teacher)
*Lord Meitreya	The main retreat is over the Confucius Temple. He also has a retreat at Varanasi, India.
*Lord Melchizedek	Guam, Vietnam.

*There are seven important retreats to visit for ascension.

1. Archangel Sandalphon at the magical crystal cave in Guatemala.
2. Mother Mary at Lourdes.
3. Archangel Metatron at Luxor.
4. Lord Voosloo at Stonehenge.
5. Archangel Butalyl at the Pyramids.
6. Lord Meitreya at the Confucius Temple, China.
7. Lord Melchizedek at Guam, Vietnam

Section Four

Nature, Animals, Stars

Chapter Forty Five

Nature

Does nature affect your ascension?

Humans are so influenced by nature that it is important to understand how it can support you on every level. If you are cut off from trees, grass, birds, flowers, their cosmic energy is not available to you. You become disconnected from Mother Earth and are starved. However, if you actively engage with the earth, the woodlands, mountains and waters, their prana and wisdom can enrich you physically as well as spiritually.

Who looks after the nature kingdom?

Archangel Purlimiek is in charge of nature for the angelic hierarchy. There are also elemental masters in charge of its different aspects.

Who is the master in charge of storms, hurricanes, earthquakes, forest fires, tsunamis or floods?

Behind all movements of nature you need a strategist who is the operations manager. The great master Poseidon, who was one of the first High Priests of the Golden Age of Atlantis after whom the Temple of Poseidon was named and who became a God in Greek mythology, is like a politician, who discusses and plans.

How is a storm raised?

Poseidon may decide that a storm needs to be raised to cleanse certain areas. He passes this information to Dom, the Elemental Master of the air, who gives commands to the sylphs, who are the air elementals. The elementals obey but they get out of control when the emotions of people attach to them. Then the angels come in to protect humans and nature, which is why you often see angels of protection during extreme weather conditions.

How are earthquakes planned?

Lady Gaia, is in charge of the earth of the Earth and her soul encapsulates the planet. She is a throne, one of the highest of the angelic hierarchy. If an earthquake is needed, for example to clear deeply entrenched negative energy from an area or to spiritually wake up the people who live there, Poseidon and Lady Gaia will consult and take the decision together. Both give the command to the earth elementals, the gnomes, pixies, imps, fairies and goblins, who act on them.

What about floods and tsunamis?

Waters are great cleansers and purifiers, though it may not seem so if your house has been flooded. At an emotional and psychic level this element washes the old away. So if Poseidon decides to create a flood he will give his orders to the elemental master Neptune. Neptune in turn will command the water elementals, the mermaids, water sprites and kyhils. He also organises wuryls, the elementals who look after the spirits. The elementals will move the waters.

Who orchestrates forest fires?

Poseidon plans the strategy and passes it to Thor, the fire elemental master. He in turn commands the salamanders. If people in countries vulnerable to forest fires would learn to connect with the salamanders, fires would only be raised for cleansing and regeneration. The devastation that is sometimes seen when elementals get out of control would be a thing of the past.

Can humans affect the ferocity of a storm?

Yes. Your thoughts and emotions have a tremendous impact. The elementals receive their commands to clear and cleanse an area and will do so forcefully but respectfully. However they are open to the thoughts and emotions of people, so human fear whips them up into a frenzy. That is when there is great damage.

Recently a great storm was forecast to hit the part of the country where I lived so I blessed and thanked the trees and flowers in my garden and sent them love. I was a little concerned about the huge trampoline that was out on the lawn for my grandchildren, but when I took a photograph during the lull before the storm, it was full of angels of protection Orbs. There were also angels of protection in front of the hedges. I asked the elementals to be gentle round my house. Then I went to bed and slept soundly. In the morning I discovered that there were trees down in the next road and quite a bit of damage to nearby houses, but my garden was untouched.

When Kathy and I were asking Archangel Michael about storms I recalled a time when I lived on a Caribbean island and a hurricane was forecast. The atmosphere became deathly quiet and black. The animals insisted on coming indoors and there was panic in the air. Stores were being looted and police cars were patrolling the streets with loudhailers warning everyone to store water. The children and I retired to a bedroom and played games. Then we all slept together in one big bed. In the morning we heard the hurricane had veered round the island. Archangel Michael told us that, even though I was spiritually unaware at the time, our calm attitude, and presumably that of enough other people, was enough to protect the island from the storm.

Chapter Forty Six

Trees and Flowers

Many people regard trees as their friends, under whom they can shelter or where they can find comfort. They may not realise that trees are keepers of ancient wisdom. They are sentient beings who know and record information about their area. They communicate with all trees in the world, so there is a vast 'tree' internet at work, sharing and storing knowledge.

When you lean against a tree or sit under one for some time with your heart open you attune to its energy and it may communicate with you. They also send healing and peace to you.

Story

Hilary and Pauline regularly used to walk on the cliff top by the ocean where they made friends with a big, very old tree. They would sit under it and really appreciate its shade. They discovered that when they were quiet, unexpected thoughts came into their minds. They wondered if the tree was telling them things. However, being scientifically trained they were very dubious about this and thought the information might be coming from their own sub-conscious minds.

One day they asked the tree to give them proof that it was talking to them. Hilary was very clairvoyant and she was immediately shown a picture of a field with a forest beyond it. Deer were running along the edge of the forest. The tree said that this was in Czechoslovakia and that the deer were in trouble.

Neither of them knew anything about deer and certainly not deer in Czechoslovakia so they wondered if they would be offered proof. Next day they were watching Country File on television and one of the items was about deer in Czechoslovakia. A film was shown of a field with a forest behind it and deer running along the edge of it. The presenter said that deer were suffering from foot rot because it had been so wet.

They could not have had a much more convincing response from their tree! They had been linked into the subtle communication of the planet to send healing to the animals.

Story

All living things, including trees respond to tides of nature. An elderly friend of mine lived as a child in Trinidad where they grew cocoa on their plantation and they wanted to plant rubber trees to provide shade for the cocoa. The wise, local overseer said, 'You can't plant rubber until the new moon,' but the boss insisted it was done that day. Nothing came up and the rubber trees had to be replanted at the following new moon.

Can trees help your ascension?

Yes, they can. When you connect with a strong healthy tree you receive subtle energy from it which raises your frequency. It can offer you healing, comfort or knowledge and link you into the oneness of nature. Certain trees protect you, so a hedge round your garden will absorb negativity from your neighbours. Others heal by taking the vibration of your pain and passing it through their roots into the earth for transmutation. They also brings down higher energy into you.

Take any opportunities you have to walk in a wood or forest, for the trees will help you in many ways and support your ascension.

How can you help your plants?

Obviously plants and seeds need water and physical nourishment in the form of good soil. They need appropriate sun and shade. But they also need prana; divine life force which is why it helps them enormously when you bless them and send them love. When you take care of their physical and spiritual needs your plants will offer you luxuriant growth and beautiful flowers or nourishing food.

They, and the elementals who look after them, respond to spiritual frequencies. While Kathy and I were in my conservatory talking to Archangel Michael about Mother Mary, I watched elementals, who are normally shy, come out of the hedge as if they were listening. I am sure they were absorbing the energy.

Is it spiritually acceptable to eat plants?

Yes. Plants evolve in many ways, one of which is through service to humanity. When you bless a plant before you cut, cook or eat it, it helps you and the entire plant kingdom.

What do flowers do for us?

Flowers offer us much more than we realise. Fairies are sweet, pure and innocent but they also have great responsibilities and powers. They accept energy from angels and unicorns and hold it steady to help people and the nature kingdom. They also place certain of these energies into the flowers.

Every colour that radiates through a bloom carries angelic love energy that has been passed down from the archangels. Fairies pour this colour into the plant, which in turn radiates it into the ethers. You have the opportunity to take in this angelic light simply by looking at it. You can ingest it more deeply by breathing it in. If you are an artist, the act of painting a flower with gratitude and intention, draws the love essence of the colour into you. A happy gardener is creating a two way transference of energy.

In countries that have seasons flowers bloom when people need their essence. In the winter there are red berries to offer a boost of life force. Then white snowdrops bring purification and hope. At the start of spring, yellow is predominant for it is the colour of sunshine and awakening. Bluebells lift the energy to the third eye once the awakening has taken place. Then there is a riot of colour throughout the summer, which subdues into subtle oranges and reds as the leaves turn in the autumn. Naturally you are drawn to the flower colours you need at any time.

Green grass and leaves are sending out healing, balancing energy at all times of the year.

How do flowers help your ascension?

It is very difficult to remain spiritually connected and ascend while living in a concrete jungle. Many of the current problems in the world are caused by people being disconnected from nature. Plants and flowers not only offer you pure light. They also give you healing and the specific energy you need at any time to assist your ascension.

Flowers at funerals help not only the mourners but the soul of the person who has died. The angels can take the essence of the flowers and use it to help the spirit on the other side. This accelerates their journey into the light and, if they are almost there, may enable them to ascend.

Chapter Forty Seven

Animals

Animals can help us with ascension. They give us love and devotion and serve our spiritual path. I discovered this for myself thanks to the tigers.

The Cat Family

All felines, including the big ones, tigers, lions, leopards, panthers and others, originate from Orion, which is considered to be the planet of wisdom. They carry qualities of enlightenment and are very psychic. They see spirits and energies, give healing and protect those they are connected to. Domestic cats look after their families, protecting them from unwanted spirits and entities. When you see a cat staring intently at something invisible to you, it is watching a spirit. If it is a visiting loved one, your cat will simply observe but if it is a malicious or unwanted entity you may see its fur stand on end. It may even hiss at the threat. It can call on protective forces and will take care of you. Your family cat is also trying to maintain the frequency in the house as high as possible.

While household cats guard the home from psychic intrusion, big ones watch over and protect our planet. Because they are highly enlightened beings they also anchor their frequency on Earth to help it to maintain its light levels. They incarnate here for an earth experience and are also wild creatures with animal instincts. However, they are not here to learn as most of us are but are teaching qualities of dignity, courage, female power, independence and enlightenment. We humans have decimated the big cat population without compassion or understanding of the true consequences for the planet.

The Tiger Temple

Early in 2008 I went to Thailand for a holiday. We had heard of the Wat Pa Luangata Bua monastery where the monks have created a wildlife sanctuary where injured animals brought to them are lovingly treated and allowed to roam freely in the grounds, then are returned to the wilds when they are ready. It is known as the tiger temple because they take in and look after tiger cubs whose mothers have been killed by poachers. They are welcomed and tended with devotion, with the consequence that they have flourished and reproduced.

Inevitably the Temple needed money to house and feed the growing tiger family. At the same time the Abbot felt that people needed to meet the great creatures for themselves and learn what love can do. After meditating he bravely decided to open the sanctuary to visitors.

We were determined to visit the sanctuary and our first glimpse was of three fluffy four week old cubs playing in the sand with their handlers. Other tigers lay nonchalantly around and we were warned not to walk in front of them but we could touch them from behind. There were many other safety warnings.

I walked down to the canyon beside the oldest tiger, a huge male. One of my hands was firmly on his back and I could feel his strength. Later I sat on the ground and cradled his huge, magnificent head on my lap. As we sat together I telepathically thanked him for his service in looking after our planet. Suddenly he raised his head and looked round, as if seeking the source of the communication. This alarmed the Abbot, who was with me in an instant, pulling the tiger off me and settling him down again! But I felt thrilled.

Later my guide, Kumeka, said that the angels had sent me there to give the tiger the message. He had indeed received it and was greatly heartened by it. It gave him hope.

A couple of weeks later my friend Heather, a wonderful old lady who has been psychic since childhood phoned me. She said that as she was quietly sitting she felt a fluffy bundle on her lap and when she looked at it she saw it was the most gorgeous little tiger cub. She was told its name was Kulah and it was sent by the spiritual hierarchy as a gift for me to assist my spiritual progress. She could not wait to tell me and I was thrilled. Kulah has been with me from that moment, playing with me and helping me.

A few days later I was taking photographs from my back door during a rain storm and there were many Orbs. One contained the spirit of the tiger cub and you can see his face in it. Kumeka immediately told me that it was my tiger cub, who had come to show himself physically to me.

Picture 44

Diana Cooper

Kulah, the tiger cub

When you look at Orb (44) you receive the knowing that animals in spirit who love you are with you as you walk your ascension path.

***

Cows

Cattle originate from Lakuma, an ascended planet round Sirius and they have incarnated to learn and teach about solid groundedness and selfless giving. Their generosity is boundless and humans have traded on their good nature.

Cows demonstrate the feminine qualities of caring and devotion, while bulls show us masculine power and protection.

Animals are very knowing. A friend lunches regularly at a pub in the New Forest, Hampshire where there are often horses, donkeys and even the occasional cow wandering freely. One day as she lunched she was amazed to see a whole herd of cows standing by the road. One even came up to the window by which she was sitting and put its face up to the glass to look at her. Her companion asked the pub landlord what was going on as she had never seen anything like it. He said,

'The farmer who owns the herd of cows died and the funeral was this morning. The hearse has just passed down the road'. Clearly the cows knew and had come to say goodbye.

Archangel Fhelyai

There is an Archangel who works particularly with animals on Earth, Archangel Fhelyai (pronounced Felyay). He continues to work with them when they return to the spirit world.

He gives animals healing directly, or through humans who have healing powers.

Archangel Fhelyai helps humans to connect to the highest level of animals, which is where they give healing and bring much happiness. If we see an animal as a dirty, smelly or inferior creature, we are untouched by their magnificence. It is when we link into their love, trust, devotion, caring and sheer majesty that they trigger our ascension potential.

The person who truly loves their dog or cat has opened doorways to oneness. This happens too if you are watching an animal and you tune into the divine glory of who it truly is. Animals are our great teachers.

Animal Ascension

Picture 45

Eugenie Morton

Archangel Christiel with Kumeka. Archangel Gabriel and an angel of love. Archangel Jophiel

When you look at picture (45) you receive the inner peace that enables you to rise above life's challenges.

Picture (45) was taken by Eugenie Morton in Custer State park in South Dakota. The message is that animals are on their own spiritual journey and that they ascend. There is a tiny Orb of Archangel Jophiel on the calf's crown. The archangel is helping him to find his life purpose, which then becomes his journey to ascension. The life purpose of cattle is to develop qualities such as tranquillity, patience and divine feminine wisdom. This particular calf is developing qualities of leadership, so that he can trust his instinct and lead his herd into safe pastures where the animals can experience freedom from fear.

The Orb to the left is a very active Kumeka with Archangel Christiel. Kumeka is making sure that the environment is safe, quiet and undisturbed while Archangel Jophiel works with the calf. Archangel Christiel is protecting Kumeka and holding the consciousness of the animals still.

The big Orb in the top middle is Archangel Gabriel and an angel of love. Archangel Gabriel is radiating purification to the plain where the animals are grazing, while the angel of love is pouring love onto them.

There are also lots of spirit Orbs and small angels of love in the picture.

***

Archangel Fhelyai

Archangel Fhelyai with an angel of love

When you look at Orb (46) you receive a 'knowing' about how important the love of animals is for your ascension.

The magnificent Orb (46) is an angel of love with Archangel Fhelyai (pronounced Felyay) who works partly with animals on Earth and partly with them when they return to the spirit world. We have cut out and enlarged this particular Orb, which was one of several wonderful pictures send to us by Patti McCullough. In the original photograph, Archangel Fhelyai appears by her dog to help it. He helps humans to connect to the highest potential of animals, which is the level at which they give healing and bring much happiness.

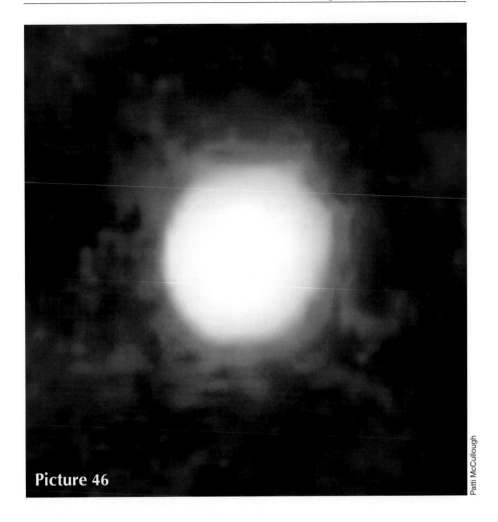

Picture 46

Patti McCullough

Chapter Forty Eight

The Stars and how they impact on the Planet

Earth is just one small planet in one galaxy among thousands, in one universe of twelve universes. Yet our tiny world is very important in the great divine plan, for Earth is the heart centre of our galaxy. Unless we all open our hearts, raise our consciousnesses and ascend, the ripples will extend far beyond our planet. If Earth does not survive, it will impact on the entire galaxy and ultimately the universe. It is time for divine love and light to return everywhere and this is not just brotherhood/sisterhood on Earth. We must accept our connection with all sentient beings in the universe.

The beings on Orion, Sirius, the Pleiades and Neptune are intimately connected with the ascension of Earth and are helping us tremendously. They access us through all the Pyramids and are pouring higher spiritual information and wisdom as well as healing onto us. In addition there are thousands of stars and planets linked to us through the universal web of light, all pulsing energy to us, mostly wanting and willing us to ascend.

When the High Priests and Priestesses left Atlantis at the fall, they took with them the knowledge about how to create pyramids and worked with the angels in their new locations to build them. A few still survive in physical form. Others still have an energetic influence.

The High Priests and Priestesses were:

Thoth who took his tribe to South America, to establish the Incas, who also built Machu Picchu.

Isis went to South America to build the Aztecs.

Horus went to Babylon.

Ra went to Egypt to seed the Pharoahs and built the Sphinx as well as pyramids.

Sett founded the Innuit culture

Imhotep formed the Native American culture.

Hermes went to Hawaii to form the Kahunas.

Zeus created the Tibetan culture.

Aphrodite created the Mayans.

Apollo went to Mesopotamia.

Poseidon went to Greece.

Hera created the Maori culture.

There is much more information about these tribes in my book *Discover Atlantis.*

Archangel Butyalil

We are not only related energetically, planet to planet. Souls from all these places have incarnated here now to anchor the light of their plane of existence on Earth. Most of these beings vibrate at a higher frequency than we do and are endeavouring to raise our consciousness. Everything is moving and flowing in a great cosmic sea and the great tidal impulse is carrying us towards the frequency of Source.

Archangel Butyalil is in charge of keeping all these cosmic currents and movements in balance for our planet as it rises towards ascension. He is working with Archangel Purlimiek of the nature kingdoms and Archangel Gersisa of the earth kingdoms as well as with the many archangels in charge of other planets who do similar work for their own region. As an ambassador for Earth, Archangel Butyalil works with them all and is helped by the unicorns.

It was Archangels Purlimiek and Butyalil who recently invited new elementals into the sphere of Earth to accelerate the purification process.

Archangel Metatron is also working with Archangel Butyalil. They are helping to make the conditions right for you to move towards opening your Stellar Gateway chakra.

Picture 47

Stuart and Audrey Mackie

Archangels Zadkiel and Christiel
with an angel of love bring an ankh

When you look at Orb (47) you receive an invitation to go to the Great Pyramid to access information for your ascension journey.

This amazing picture (47) containing the symbol of an ankh was taken by Stuart and Audrey Mackie a few seconds after they had asked if the white lights were "positive" spirit. It was the first and only shot that they got that night.

The angel of love is inviting you, with love, to enter the ankh within it, which is a portal. Archangel Zadkiel is transmuting any negative energy so that it is safe for you to enter. And Archangel Christiel, who is in charge of the development of the causal chakra, is helping your mind to be still and quiet, so that you can experience a journey for your highest good.

The ankh contains the wisdom of Egypt, Atlantis and Lemuria and you can go through it to access gifts you had in those ancient times of interstellar communication and cosmic wisdom.

When you go into the ankh you find yourself in the chamber of light in the Great Pyramid, and you must go through several purification experiences to ensure that you are ready when you reach it. Here you receive healing from the four planets and also access information specific to your ascension journey. There are many different pathways which lead from this chamber. Some of these are interstellar and take you to the four planets which are influencing the ascension of Earth – the Pleiades, Orion, Sirius and Neptune. The other paths are on Earth. Archangel Christiel, who carries the protective Christ ray, will lead you onto the right one for you.

***

Seraphim with Beings from Orion

When you look at Orb (48) you receive a sense of the grace of the universe.

When we saw Orb (48) we gasped, for the aliens surrounded by the Seraphim are so clear. When we asked about this Orb we were told that years ago beings from Orion came to Earth to bring enlightenment to humanity. The people were terrified and through nasty intent and ignorance locked the spirits of the aliens into the rock of the mountain.

The Orb is the Seraphim, Seraphiel, who has arrived under grace to help the spirit of the mountain. Several of these mightiest of angels came to Earth for

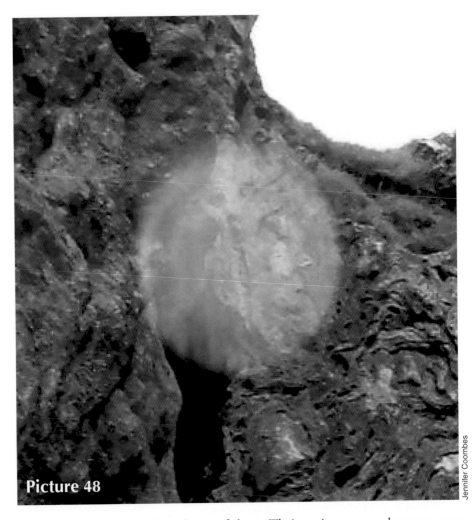

Picture 48

Jennifer Coombes

this task and we have enlarged one of them. Their main purpose, however, was to release the wise ones who have been locked into the rock all this time. It is an awesome privilege and not by chance that humanity has been allowed to witness this moment.

Conclusion

Orbs are the light bodies of angelic beings. By impressing themselves onto film they are giving you an unprecedented opportunity to receive their light, their messages, invitations and teachings directly into your unconscious. This is the second book in the series. *Enlightenment Through Orbs* is the first and we are guided to write *Healing Through Orbs* next.

By opening your heart and raising your vibration you can take your own Orb pictures. Then you can help to raise the consciousness of everyone by sharing them.

We have been told by the spiritual hierarchy that working with certain Orbs offers one of the fastest pathways to ascension and we can believe it. The months during which we were writing *Ascension Through Orbs* were awesome and we buzzed with excitement and pure energy as we explored particular Orbs and experienced their messages.

This particular period in the history of the planet offers opportunities for ascension that have not been available since the time of Golden Atlantis. We hope that you too are touched by the light of the Orbs and accept their invitation to ascend in this lifetime.

We wish you love, joy and angel blessings,
Diana Cooper and Kathy Crosswell

The time is now.
Earth is ascending.
Let us take this opportunity to raise our
frequency and assist the ascension process.

Meditations with the Orbs and exercises to aid your Ascension

This section is offered to you for your enjoyment. Each of the meditations has been channelled through Kathy from Wywyvsil. They will help you attune to the message related to each picture and will support you to make steps forward on your ascension pathway. Not all the channelled meditations have been included within this book. They are available at www.kathycrossswell.com or www.healingorbs.com.

In addition Kathy has shared her very personal experiences as she has 'entered' many of the Orbs. She is always very excited when she returns from her journey and she offers some tips on how you too could enjoy the feeling and 'being' of the Orbs. Each and every time the experience is different, depending on so many factors at the time. The one thing that is consistent is that Kathy knows each time that she has grown spiritually and that she has taken another step on her ascension pathway.

Tips to enter the Orbs

Every Orb is different and therefore they will bring a completely unique experience to you. It is also important to recognise that you are an individual and so each encounter will be just for you. Also every time you enter the Orb it will be different again as you will have progressed and the Orb may be supporting others too.

There are so many ways to link with the beings in the Orbs. Remember they are 'windows' to the beings in the higher realms and are always open for you to reach out to them.

It is always important that you bring yourself to a good place before you link with the 'Orbs' to ensure you maximise each visit. To do this it is worth practicing the following and to make this your disciplined routine:

1. Cleanse the area before you start. Picture a blue light and pull it down through the area (house or room). You should feel the energy change to a higher vibration and this often feels like it is electric or tingling. When it has completely filled the space and has reached the ground, then take the

energy back up and out to the universe to be transmuted. The energy will become lighter, fresher and calm.

2. Cleanse yourself by drawing white light through your feet gradually and steadily up through the whole of your body and then back down through your body. Make sure you offer again your energy to the universe to transmute.

3. Ask Archangel Michael to protect your area. Imagine a very strong blue bubble around you.

4. Light a candle for the greater good of all.

5. Find a comfortable place to sit.

6. Breathe in the wonderful energy offered from the Earth and the universe making sure you hold this in your solar plexus.

7. Push the 'held' energy from your solar plexus up and down through your chakras and out into your aura.

8. 'Enter' the Orbs. These ideas may work for you.

a. Picture the Orb in your mind and then push out your aura to enclose the Orb picture.

b. Ask the 'beings' in the Orb to expand their energy and enclose you.

c. Sit with your eyes open and look at the Orb and picture in your mind being within the Orb. This is not exhaustive and with a little practice you will find your own way.

9. You may not know you are in the Orb for a while. It does take a bit of practice to feel the subtleties. I know I am very lucky to be clairsentient as this certainly helps, so please don't give up if you don't notice anything immediately. That said, I have practiced many different approaches to entering the Orbs within my workshops and I have not come across a person who cannot do this.

10. The most important tip I can give you is to really enjoy the experience. Feel all the emotions, recall the visual scenes and messages you are given. Each encounter will be for you.

11. When the vision starts to get wobbly, or you lose the connection emotionally then it is time to bring your breathing back to its normal state.

12. Thank those who you have met and who have helped you.

13. Stand up, shake your energy and give it to the universe

14. Thank Archangel Michael for the protection.

15. Record your encounter; it will be relevant to you at some point.

The most important tip I can give you is **do not** put yourself under pressure. If you are not successful immediately, don't worry. Remember you are being guided and when the timing is right then you will enter the window easily. Go with the flow.

Picture 1 (Chapter 1) – Receive an invitation to the Seventh Heaven

Exercise to bring love and light to things you do

This is an exercise most of us need to practise. It can help your relationships and change your life.

1. Sit and look at the picture (1) for a moment.
2. Light a candle and dedicate it to bringing love and light to the world.
3. Think of something you really love doing. This can be anything.
4. Really focus on this activity, but make sure you are filling it with love and light.
5. Keep this focus pure and as long as you can sustain it.
6. Know completely that you have been successful.
7. Relax and thank Mary Magdelene, El Morya and Serapis Bey for their support.

Picture 2 (Chapter 3) – Receive angelic assistance to help you set your loved ones free

Exercise to support you to let those you love grow

1. Look at picture (2) of the unicorn and angel of love.
2. Focus on a loved one you know you are having difficulty letting go and name them out loud if possible, or think it very clearly.
3. Ask the unicorn to take away the fear within you which is causing you to behave this way.
4. State emphatically, 'I give to you the fear I have which I am using to hold back my loved one'.
5. Breathe in to your heart chakra the love from the angel of love and into your solar plexus a ball of golden light to transmute your fear.
6. Do this as many times as you need to, to release those you love from your fear.

Picture 3 (Chapter 3) – receive permission to be yourself wherever you are, so that you can walk the ascension pathway as yourself.

Kathy shares her experience of what it is like to join with Archangel Raphael's energy. She has written this as it occurred:

As I am sitting here I feel my heart chakra vibrating at a quicker rate than is usual. I know my throat chakra is changing as it does for channelling. My breathing becomes very shallow. I sense an Orb in front of me enveloping my heart and crown chakras. I know I am looking at a very green Orb. It is textured, and in its centre is a point – a dot, yet I know there is more to this dot.

From the centre flows many circles, each vibrating slightly less energetically than the first. It is transparent and green at the same time. You can see through it and you can't. The outer circle, which surrounds the Orb, is firm and protective and vibrating at a lower vibration. Around it is an aura, which is infinite and it is this I feel at the moment. The energy is calming and healing and it quietens me. It makes me relaxed and it puts me in a place ready to link well and receive intuition. It knows I am looking at it and it is waiting for me to be ready to receive it. It knows I am curious about it. I now feel I want to know more and it responds by 'coming to life' again. I am now consumed by the Orb and I am in its energy.

I cannot see out now, yet I was expecting to be able to do so. The energy is very high and I am vibrating with its energy and I am part of it. It has a depth, is infinite and links firmly to the source of the universe. I am completely relaxed and at peace. I have an urge to ask it to take away my headache.

Immediately I yawn, choke and when I recover my headache has gone. I feel this Orb's purpose is to bring abundance to the universe. It brings this energy to all without any expectations. I could journey with this Orb for hours. It resonates with my vibrations easily. It draws on the purest energy and can fragment this energy into infinite Orbs as needed. It will surround everything, planets, people, and nature – whatever, wherever and whenever this is needed.

It pushes out its aura to ensure cosmic inspiration can be heard and understood and where required, healing can be felt. When called upon this Orb will come to you and through meditation, abundance, healing and clarity can be achieved.

Archangel Raphael clarifies abundance as pure happiness, pure fulfilment and peace – a quietness of the soul. He tells me that through working with his energy he will raise my abundance consciousness to help me bring enlightenment and spiritual growth to as many people as possible.

Exercise to be yourself wherever you are

1. Look at picture (3) of Archangels Uriel and Raphael.
2. Light a candle and dedicate it to love.
3. Stand up and say very proudly 'I give me permission to be me'.
4. Jump around and shout loudly 'I love being me'.
5. Say loudly, 'In the name of God I invoke an angel of love to come to me.'

6. Trust that this has been done.
7. Jump around again and allow the light to enter you.
8. Know that others will see your glow and want to be part of it.

Picture 4 (Chapter 3) – activates enlightenment that takes you on your path to ascension

Exercise to bring forward your inner child

1. Sit and look at picture (4).
2. Hold a picture in your head of when you were a child having fun, or watch a child playing and sense how much they are enjoying themselves.
3. Say out loud, 'I call on Archangel Michael to bring me courage to remember to bring forward my inner child'.
4. Know with complete certainty that this has happened
5. Draw these feelings into your heart chakra and hold them there.
6. Share this pure energy with as many people as you can.

Picture 5 (Chapter 3) – receive a clearance of your consciousness that will enable you to move out of your limited space onto an ascension pathway

Kathy shares her experience of what it is like to join with Archangel Uriel's energy. She has written this as it occurred:

Uriel holds your vision to allow connection to occur and his energy is very different from the other Orbs. It is malleable and fluid and is like 'trying to land on jelly' which is at full wobble. This is because he absorbs energy and changes consistently to allow this to happen. Inside the Orb I can feel opportunity is everywhere and I see things, similar to ley lines stretching away into the distance. Each of these carry the essence of him to us and takes our impurities away to be transmuted. The texture is very complex. It looks like a sponge with millions of small pockets where negativity is held. At his brightest, Archangel Uriel is golden yellow, vibrant and clear, but when full and ready to transmute, the Orb will appear dim and taupe in colour. When I was melding with the Orb, I was not permitted into any of the pockets for risk of collecting negativity.

The lines felt like carbon, they do not transmute electricity and the magnetic pull of Earth does not affect these Orbs. When they are transmuting negative energy these lines become active and change from carbon textured to pure crystal raising the vibration and consciousness within. At the climax of the transmutation the Orbs 'explode' showering golden light as far as is possible. As quickly as these 'explosions' occur, they are ready to start over again.

Exercise to clear your consciousness

1. Light a candle and dedicate it to successfully clearing your consciousness and moving you forward on your pathway to ascension.
2. Sit quietly and close your eyes.
3. Draw your energy up from the Earth and down from the Universe and ensure it is held in your solar plexus.
4. As you are sitting there ask Archangel Uriel to remove any negative energy from you.
5. Ask Archangel Raphael to heal the impact of this energy.
6. Ask Archangel Zadkiel to help you approach situations in a positive way in the future.
7. Offer to the universe this energy to be transmuted for the greater good.
8. Sit for a moment quietly.
9. Thank Archangels Uriel, Raphael and Zadkiel for their support.
10. Blow out the candle.

Picture 6 (Chapter 4) – receive a feeling that everything is alright

Exercise to be assured that everything is alright

1. Look at picture (6) for a few moments.
2. Light a candle and dedicate it to receiving a sense of assurance about who you are.
3. Sit quietly and focus on your heart chakra. Breathe love into it and peace out of it.
4. Visualise yourself with a huge pink aura.
5. Imagine a circumstance that you are worried about.
6. Know that Lone Wolf has surrounded you in confidence and recognise how good this feels.
7. Know that whatever the outcome, the result will be for the greater good of all those involved.
8. Thank him very much.

Picture 7 (Chapter 4) - receive a knowing that you are guided

Meditation – for the planet and for yourself

You find yourself as a child staring out of a window. It is raining hard and you have your nose pressed against the pane of glass, feeling how chilled it is. Outside it is cold, dull and very wet and windy and this makes you shiver a little. It is so fascinating watching the water drops as they land on the window and race each other to the bottom. One of the drops in particular catches your eye. It is beautiful as it is full of colour, purple, blue, silver and pink. You close your eyes to hold the picture of this rain drop in your mind and, for that moment, you forget about the rain. As you open your eyes you are now completely enclosed in a purple mist and the rain has gone. You are standing on grass. As your eyes adjust to this purple hue you begin to realise you are in the middle of Stonehenge.

It is not raining here. You sit cross legged to soak in the atmosphere and with that decision the purple mist expands to enclose the stones too. Suddenly, you are aware of a presence, a man, who is walking round wafting a fragrance from a bowl. He is very old indeed. He is one of the ancient wise men who have come to invite you to join him as he takes you to a place of higher consciousness. You are humbled and excited to go with him. He walks up to you and places the bowl at your feet and takes your hands in his. He looks you in the eyes and immediately you begin to feel your aura expanding.

You know your chakras are tingling and you particularly sense activity in the crown chakra. You begin to rise from your physical frame and immediately your energy expands further. You are able to sense from the stones a little of the history of Stonehenge. As his energy entwines with yours, you again notice a shift in consciousness as you are now aware of how the planet felt at that moment. As he expands your energy even further you become acutely aware of what you *must* do for the planet and for yourself to maintain and continue to ascend. There is no doubt. You get an urgency to return to your physical frame to get on with these tasks. He holds your energy for a moment longer to allow the purple mist to enclose you again, bringing your energy back to your physical dimension. As this occurs you find yourself sitting comfortably in your home, full of desire and determination to continue on your ascension pathway.

Visualisation to help you see you are guided

When you ask a spiritual being to do something, you can assist them by visualising it being accomplished.

1. Look at picture (7).
2. Light a candle.
3. Picture you safe, happy and well.
4. Place your request to the angelic hierarchy and visualise this occurring.
5. Ask your guardian angel to enfold you in their wings and imagine this happening.
6. Ask Archangel Michael with his sword and shield to stand by you and protect you. Picture this as clearly as you can.

7. Ask Archangel Gabriel to give you clarity.
8. Know Archangel Zadkiel will transmute your energy and bring you vitality and life force.
9. Thank Archangels Michael, Gabriel and Zadkiel for their support.

Picture 8 (Chapter 5) – receive healing and a desire to bring oneness to the world.

Visualisation to bring oneness to the world

1. Find a place where you can be quiet and undisturbed.
2. Look at picture (8) then close your eyes and relax by focusing on love as you breathe in and peace as you breathe out.
3. Think of a place in the world which would benefit from healing and peace
4. Visualise a unicorn Orb on your crown chakra opening you to your higher self.
5. Picture the unicorn and two angels of love coming to this place.
6. Visualise them bringing healing, relax into the feeling this brings you.
7. Know that this healing will start to bring peace to this place.
8. Thank the spiritual hierarchy for the help they are bringing to the world.

Picture 9 (Chapter 5) – receive enlightenment about just how much help is available to humanity.

Receive another level of enlightenment

1. Look at picture (9).
2. Say the following invocation to Archangel Gabriel aloud:
3. 'I now dedicate myself to enlightenment and invoke the mighty Archangel Gabriel to enable me to see everything and everyone with the eyes of spirit.'
4. Close your eyes and feel Archangel Gabriel touching your third eye.
5. Ask Archangel Gabriel to show you how much help is available to humanity.
6. Relax deeply and allow an expansion of consciousness to take place, to embed how you too can help humanity.
7. Open your eyes and thank Archangel Gabriel.
8. Consciously change your attitude to everything and everyone.

Picture 10 (Chapter 5) – receive freedom to move into an expanded life.

Meditation - broadening your perspective on life, because you love life
You find yourself as a cave dweller many years ago. You are very adept at survival

skills, making good use of all the local vegetation for both food and shelter. You are also very fit and healthy. You don't venture far from your cave as you have everything you need for your well-being in the immediate surroundings. One day however, you wake up and there has been a fire. Everything has been burnt to the ground and all your wonderful food has gone. You are very upset but you don't panic, instead you set off on an exploration.

You are feeling really good about this change. You walk into the sun as this makes you feel better until you find a beautiful, ancient and spreading tree and decide to take a rest and sit under it. The ground is covered in moss and very comfortable. It is lovely to just sit there and relax for a moment. As you are sitting there you spot a small rodent nudging its way through the leaves and you get up to follow it. As you do you completely lose track of where you have been and you suddenly find yourself in a clearing with the most stunningly beautiful waterfall. You have never seen anything quite like it before. You go closer and the spray hits your face, you are fascinated. As you get really close you can see there is a cave behind the waterfall and you can get into it by climbing on some of the rocks.

Once in the cave you are amazed by how big it is and how it is lit by glistening crystals in the rock. The reflection from the light through the water curtain illuminates the cave. Instantaneously, you decide you are going to stay here and not return to the cave you have inhabited for all your life. You are filled with the spirit of adventure. You sit down behind the waterfall and smile. As you are sitting there you close your eyes and breathe in the purity of the air. When you open your eyes you realise completely that you will never stop broadening your perspective on life, because you love life!

Exercise to receive freedom to expand your life

1. Look at picture (10).
2. Imagine you are sitting under the tree and you are bathed in the energy given by Seraphiel and Paul the Venetian.
3. Ask them to bring this energy to you and completely enfold you in it.
4. Feel it enter each of your cells and purifying you. Take note of any changes this brings for you.
5. Imagine your mind opening to new opportunities.
6. Ask the angels to bring these to you, knowing that they will only be fulfilled if you have acknowledged that this is right for you and for the greater good of all.
7. Thank them for their work on your behalf.
8. Keep breathing in the higher consciousness and be open to the new opportunities.

Picture 11 (Chapter 6) – receive a reminder that there are many stuck or lost souls who will be drawn to your light. Remember them and protect yourself.

Kathy shares her experience of what it is like to join with Archangel Gabriel's energy. She has written this as it occurred:

As I sit with this Orb I can immediately feel my third eye and crown chakras expanding. I sense that I have 360° 'vision'. I know I am inside it and that I am seeing everywhere at once. In fact my rear view vision appears brighter and more active than that which is front of me. There is a bright light surrounding me now and I am aware that I am held in Archangel Gabriel's energy. I know that now is the time to ask any questions I might need to have answered, for I am held in a state of energy conducive to receiving clarity.

The light diminishes and I can see that Archangel Gabriel's texture is a very fine mesh, extremely strong, flexible and gentle. It surrounds the Orb, yet inside it is liquid and quite fragrant. Although I can't quite find the words to describe the scent, I like it but I don't know what it is. Once in the liquid I find I am being moved along purposefully. After a while my cells feel as if they are the liquid. I know they are being healed and with this I will be able to see things more clearly. I can sense the Orb knows I am interested and curious and it is happy for me to explore it. Although it looks small, it is not. It is expansive and it would appear to be able to support an infinite amount of people who might need clarity. As I am 'held' in the liquid, its energy, something amazing happens. I am no longer moving; in fact the liquid holding me has stopped, but everything around me now moves at speed.

I feel as if I am in a still and tranquil pool next to a fast flowing river. Again, I see the bright light now in the distance and where the fluid is flowing to. I immediately sense other 'beings' now in the Orb and I am permitted to see that these souls have been rescued and are now held in a suspended state and offered the option of the clarity I was privileged to have been party to earlier.

I am also aware that working through Archangel Gabriel is Archangel Raphael's energy offering healing to these souls. This is quite an intense and awe inspiring moment for these souls. I am stunned that the energy in the Orb is so lively and moveable. It is so hard to summarise what I am really seeing as it can be at rest one moment and expanding to hold souls the next. Truly outstanding!

Exercise to bring love to lost souls

1. Light a candle and dedicate it to all lost souls.
2. Sit quietly and ask Archangel Michael to protect you.

3. Regulate your breathing, ensuring that you are drawing energy from Mother Earth and the universe into your heart chakra.

4. Allow this energy to permeate your soul.

5. Expand your aura as far as you can, reaching out to souls who are lost.

6. Close your eyes and sense them.

7. Offer up your love and light to those souls who need to be guided to the light.

8. Ask Archangel Michael to protect them.

9. Ask Archangel Gabriel to help them see that they can clearly move into the light.

10. Know that this has been done and that they will continue to receive love and light.

11. Cleanse your aura by bringing a ball of white light up through your feet, legs, torso, arms, and head and bring it back down again.

12. Offer up this energy to be transmuted and given to the universe.

Picture 12 (Chapter 7) – receive a sense of fairness of the universe

Meditation – see how beautiful nature is.

You find yourself in a garden. It is in full bloom and the colour and smell sends all your senses into overdrive. You are lying down enjoying the sunshine. At that moment you have no worries at all. Your eye catches a glimpse of a honey bee busy at work. You sit up to watch it more closely. The bee is a beautiful colour and so agile. It flits between the flower heads, and you marvel at how it dips itself into the wonderful nectar in each of the flowers. The skill it has to fly with such accuracy and to hold so still to gather in nature's precious delicacies is inspiring.

It also makes a soothing hum as it is flying and this gets even louder when it hovers. Each time the bee emerges from the depth of a flower head you can see it has more and more nectar in its pouches which hang from each side of the bee. Whilst you are observing this you become aware that you are gently bathed in Archangel Christiel's energy. With this, your vision begins to change and you can suddenly see in a way you have never been able to before. As well as watching the bee you can see the energy around the flowers and the bee. The flowers are colourful and fragrant to attract the bee and their energy is pushed right out and shining brightly too. It looks amazing. As the bee is drinking the nectar the flowers gradually retract their energy.

You can sense the flowers feel great but also spent, as if they had just run a race and won. You look around the whole garden and you can see this happening everywhere and continuously. Finally, the bee turns from the flowers and now completely laden with nectar flies off into the distance. You lie down again, look to the sky and find your vision has returned to normal. You see birds flying in formation, with fluffy clouds in the sky and you know that the universe is fair and wholesome, and when left to its own devices is a magical place to be.

Visualisation to sense the fairness of the universe

1. Look at picture (12).
2. Find a place outside where you can be undisturbed.
3. Ask Archangel Christiel to show you how the elementals support a flower as it grows, from when it roots to its first bloom.
4. See clearly what is shown to you and accept this vision into your heart.
5. Feel yourself blending with the flower.
6. Visualise yourself becoming invisible as you become one with the flower.
7. See how well the flower is supported and how intricate this balance is.
8. Enjoy this moment until if gradually fades away.
9. Thank them for allowing you to experience their world.

Picture 13 (Chapter 7) – receive a deep connection with nature

Exercise to connect with nature

1. Look at picture (13).
2. Sit quietly and ask Archangel Mariel and Peter the Great to bring to you a stronger connection with nature
3. If you can, take a walk out in nature, if not look at a picture of a very beautiful scene from nature.
4. Push out your aura and feel how wonderful nature is. If you can, pick up a discarded leaf and hold it gently. Allow these great beings to connect you with nature.
5. Send them love and sense they are responding to you.
6. Feel them protecting you and keeping you safe.
7. When you leave the natural world, thank them very much.

Picture 14 (Chapter 7) – receive an acceleration of your ascension

Meditation – to meet with angels
You find yourself travelling down the road in a beautiful convertible Corvette Stingray. The roof is down. The road is long and straight and there are mountains to your left with tops covered in snow. The sun is shining and everything is

just perfect. Further down the road there are many trees with the most vibrantly coloured leaves. You are in awe of the beauty and with the wind on your face and the engine noise in your ears you feel amazing. The road ahead now begins to wind slowly up into the foothills of the mountain. The air starts to get fresher and you begin to feel cold, so you pull over to get a jumper from the back of your car.

As you are walking around admiring the scenery you are met by the most astounding sight. In front of you is an escalator surrounded by colour. The view is stunning as everywhere you look is a different shade and it is awesome. You step onto it and immediately you feel it begin to rise. As it rises you know something very special is happening. Your energy feels different and more disconnected to the physical world and more in touch with the higher dimensions. You are becoming more and more excited. Suddenly, you reach the top of the escalator, and you find yourself in a golden globe.

It is full of angels all waiting to speak with you and you take your place amongst them. Archangel Raphael and Wywyvsil start by sharing their messages with you, followed by each of the angels. With each message given, you know without a doubt that your consciousness has changed and you can see more clearly where you are. It takes quite a while for you to receive all the messages. When the last angel has given you the information you become aware you are descending and that your energy is becoming much more physical.

Eventually, you find yourself back in your comfortable place clearly a little further on your path to ascension, and very grateful to the angels for sharing their messages with you.

Exercise to receive healing and help to clear karmic issues

1. Look at photograph (14) of Wywyvsil and Archangel Raphael.
2. Sit quietly.
3. Open yourself to receive healing.
4. Ask Archangel Raphael for healing and ask Wywyvsil to bring to the fore karmic issues that you must deal with.
5. Ask for clarity and understanding to remove the karma.
6. Breathe in deeply and allow this knowledge and wisdom to enter your soul.
7. Sit quietly for a few moments.
8. Know that this has been done.
9. Be grateful and thankful for this healing and know that this will help you receive an acceleration of your ascension.

Pictures 15 and 16 (Chapter 9) – receive a boost on your ascension pathway

Receive a boost on your spiritual path

1. Look at pictures (15 and 16).
2. Feel Archangel Michael placing his blue light of protection around you.
3. Ask any question.
4. Know that Archangel Raphael will bring healing to your soul to allow you to receive the answer.
5. Archangel Gabriel will make the answer clear.
6. Archangel Gabriel will ensure the answer is held in peace.
7. Archangel Metatron is encouraging you to proceed on your spiritual path way.
8. Close your eyes and imagine you are going through your next day with all this support.
9. Know that the more you ask for inspiration, the more help you will get to ensure you receive and act on this answer from the depth of your heart.

Picture 17 (Chapter 11) – receive courage, healing and support on your ascension pathway.

Kathy shares her experience of what it is like to join with Archangel Michael and Uriel's energy. She has written this as it occurred:
This Orb has appeared to support people on the Earth plane. It has come particularly for people who are spiritually aware and who have 'Earth binding' moments, where they do not want the people they know to pass over, even though they are prepared and can accept this will happen. Archangels Uriel and Michael remove the fear which is holding them back and allow for enlightenment to occur. This brings a much greater spiritual understanding and connection.

As I combine with this Orb I am able to feel that the archangels brought courage to cope with the passing of their loved ones and the belief to strengthen their link with the spirit world. The unicorn energy is holding the spirit of the person who has passed, allowing this soul to be at peace and to have the confidence to leave their loved ones in the safe energy of Archangels Uriel and Michael. This beautiful dimensional connection has raised the consciousness of all involved in this passing. This higher understanding will continue to resonate and will also impact on others who now touch those directly involved.

Each person's energy has changed now. They are much more grounded and also more enlightened. There is quite a shift in the dimension of the Earth Star chakra. It is very important that those involved continue to link with Archangel

Uriel to further develop and strengthen the spiritual understanding as the Earth Star chakra continues to stir.

Meditation – remove your Earth binding moments
You are sad today as you have just found out that your job is coming to an end. There is a reorganisation taking place at work as savings have to be made. The company has invested in new technology which, in the long term, will bring an increase in productivity and improve the financial bottom line. You can understand why the Board of Directors has made this decision but for you it is awful. You are really worried as you have your family to support and you just don't know how you are going to achieve this now.

You decide to go for a walk at lunchtime to clear your head. As you are walking you are sending up prayers asking for support to help you see things clearly. You also ask for all the negative thoughts you are getting to be removed as soon as they appear and for healing, as you know you and your family will need it. Immediately, you begin to feel refreshed and excited. You start to see little snippets of what is to come. A sign says 'change is the best form of growth and healing'.

You also see a boy slip off his bike in front of you, and as you offer support to pick him up and see him safely on your way this too makes you feel much better. You make your way back to work quite confident that leaving this job will be 'just the ticket' to move you onto something so much better for you and your family. In fact you can't wait to know what this is. You again send up a thought to the universe and you trust completely that you will be guided to make the right choices. You find that you now have a skip in your step. You go back to work with no worries and know that your best interests are being held for your highest good.

Visualisation to receive courage, healing and support and find a sense of peace
It is very effective to do this visualisation at the new moon.
1. Find a place where you can be quiet and relaxed and look at picture (17).
2. Close your eyes and imagine you are pulling a heavily laden sleigh up a very steep hill. It contains all your doubts and lack of confidence.
3. Notice how close you are to reaching the summit but how far it seems to be. The thought of what you have to achieve is bringing you down and slowing you down.
4. Ask Archangel Michael to give you the courage to strive forward with confidence.

5. Ask Archangel Uriel to lift from you all your doubts and lack of trust. How do you feel?
6. Visualise being held in a yellow energy carrying the deepest wisdom and peace.
7. Visualise the unicorn striding proudly by your side and as you reach the summit, his light shining far and wide.
8. Visualise the sleigh, now ready to descend, empty from the burden you were carrying.
9. Mentally ask the Archangels to replace your doubts.
10. Tell them that you are now ready to access your deepest wisdom to replace the ways you have been thinking.
11. Relax deeply to allow them to start making changes within you.
12. Ensure you thank them fully.

Picture 18 (Chapter 11) – celebrate the awakening of your Earth Star chakra, which is a rite of passage to the next step of your ascension journey

Kathy shares her experience of what it is like to join with Archangels Sandalphon, Gabriel, Christiel and Mallory's energy. She has written this as it occurred:

As I look into this Orb I am amazed at how bright it is. I was not expecting this. There is a tube in the centre and it is cream in colour. I am not permitted entry at this time. I know it is waiting at the moment and I too have to wait. It is quiet, like it is sleeping. I have a very strong sense of anticipation. As I wait my breathing becomes deeper and slower. I am very relaxed. As my breathing deepens further I feel as if I am in a meditative state, calm and peaceful. Before I know it I am now consumed by this Orb.

I am in a very dense fluid; it is thick and gluey but comforting. I am able to move but only very slowly. It is definitely for relaxing and reflecting. It would be an ideal Orb to relax the soul. As I fully relax and 'become' of the Orb I realise there is so much more to it than just being relaxed. I can feel anticipation coming back again. The fluid is now gently flowing and I am moving with the flow. I am being taken further into it and it feels great.

Eventually, the fluid stops flowing and in the centre of the Orb is a grid and I know I have been in just one aspect of it. In the centre, as I step out of the fluid and onto the grid, is bright light, and I am very aware of my connection with my higher consciousness and also my grounding. I realise with certainty that I have reached a very spiritual place, where I have the opportunity to raise my energy and develop my spiritual pathway. If you meditate in this Orb it will be a very relaxed and enlightening experience.

Visualisation to celebrate the awakening of your Earth Star chakra

1. Look at picture (18).
2. Light a candle and find a space where you can be undisturbed.
3. Sit comfortably.
4. With your hands stretched high to the heavens invoke Archangel Sandalphon and see him before you offering a globe. In it is the Earth spinning in its full beauty.
5. Thank him for his gift and tell him you accept it with honour.
6. Visualise him throwing the globe to the floor with huge force so that it cracks open.
7. See before you the Earth as it is seen by the archangels; for you are every little aspect that makes up the Earth.
8. Sit within its glorious light and dedicate yourself in service to the divine. Humbly ask for assistance.
9. See before you a ball of light which is neither white nor black yet it is both. Know that this is your earth Star chakra and that you are now linked firmly to the earth and the universe.
10. Before your eyes the globe reforms to 'hold' again the Earth and this is placed carefully around your neck. Know without a doubt that your Earth Star is awake.
11. Close your eyes give thanks and enjoy the celebration light show given to you.

Picture 19 (Chapter 11) – receive a connection deep into the earth and up to heaven to assist your ascension.

Meditation – receive a breath of life from Source

You are in Luxor in the Egyptian desert. There are many people going about their business. You are not interested in what they are doing because you are strongly drawn to the largest pyramid. You are making your way over to it. There is a breeze and the sand is starting to blow gently in your face, so you turn away from the direct impact of the wind. Finally, you reach the pyramid and can feel the excitement growing and you can't wait to get inside.

Once inside you have a complete knowing of where you are. You know your way around inside the pyramid as you have definitely been here before. You have an instinct to walk to a particular chamber, sit and then wait. You settle into a meditative state and begin to rock from right to left and left to right. You also hum gently and repetitively. The atmosphere in the room becomes heavy and then it becomes alive.

There is a tremendous light and you know there is a very powerful energy running from the earth to the heavens, directly up your spine. You can also feel it returning too and as it enters the earth it enlightens the ley lines. As this occurs you know the earth has been given a breath of life from God and that you provided this. It is humbling as you realise, that if every person were to recognise their higher consciousness, the earth would heal and grow.

A prayer for the Earth

1. Look at picture (19).
2. Offer this prayer. 'In the name of God and all that is light, I ask for the love, strength, resources and a deep connection to Earth and the heavens to help the Earth to flourish. I call on Archangels Roquiel and Sandalphon, to assist me. I dedicate myself to helping and honouring our beautiful planet.'

Picture 20 (Chapter 13) – receive a feeling of alignment with the universe.

Meditation – receive a very special shower

You find yourself in the depth of a cave. It is damp, warm and lit by the hundreds of shafts of light shining through very tiny gaps in the roof. It is a beautiful cave full of stalagmites and stalactites, they are obviously thousands of years old. You stand in awe of this glorious sight. Never have you seen anything so wonderful. You move towards the back of the cave and are met by a thunderous roar and a spectacle beholds you. There is a cavern so tall you cannot see the top, with a waterfall falling from these heady heights. It crashes to the bottom with such force, the resulting spray reaches so high it is frightening. You find a rock to sit on as near as you can get to this waterfall. You are being covered in spray. It tastes so pure and it is exceptionally cold. It makes you shiver. As you are looking at this, the cavern becomes full of yellow light. The water turns a golden hue and as the spray covers you with golden sparkles, you know you have received a very special shower. Each sparkle makes you shiver and also brings your energy to a fever pitch. It is nearly too much to take, but you love it. You immediately grow in confidence and know you have been blessed with positivity. With this realisation the light dims and your energy comes back to a level you can cope with. You get up and walk away from the waterfall and back out towards the front of the cave. You are different now, mellower and content with whom you are.

Exercise to receive a shower of positivity and confidence

1. Look at the picture (20).
2. Play, hum or listen to a beautiful piece of music or singing.

3. Call in Archangel Zadkiel to hold you in positive energy.
4. Call in Archangel Uriel and ask him to shower you in the energy of the sound.
5. Call in Archangel Raphael to draw the healing of the sound into your solar plexus.
6. Visualise your solar plexus filled with golden light.
7. Watch them push this light up through your chakras and it bursting out and showering you with positivity and confidence.
8. Feel the energy moving deep within you.
9. Thank Archangels Zadkiel, Uriel and Raphael.

Picture 21 (Chapter 14) - receive love and joy and a desire to share this with others

Visualisation to share love and joy with others

1. Look at picture (21) of Archangel Chamuel.
2. Find a place where you can be quiet and relaxed.
3. Light a candle and dedicate it to the sharing of love and joy with others.
4. Close your eyes and ask Archangel Chamuel to enfold you in a beautiful soft pink cloud. It is full of love and joy.
5. Visualise everything and everyone you wish to share this experience with.
6. Now open your arms to Archangel Chamuel and let him take you to the cosmic heart.
7. Be very still and listen to the beating of the cosmic heart.
8. Visualise this soft pink cloud getting bigger and bigger as it expands to take in the full extent of the love being offered.
9. See this cloud bursting and the love and joy falling like droplets to those who need it.
10. Visualise everyone and everything starting to smile and see a lightness form in their auras.
11. Thank Archangel Chamuel for this kindness.
12. Open your eyes knowing that you can always repeat this exercise and each time you do so your life and that of others will become more love filled and joyful.

Picture 22 (Chapter 15) – receive a great boost of courage, strength and protection

Meditation – to fly safely and with protection
You find yourself flying a very small plane. You are an accomplished pilot having flown now for many years. You are on your way to visit a friend, who lives

across the sea on a small island. As you are thinking about what you will do when you meet up, you receive a call from air traffic control alerting you to a major storm ahead of you. You check your fuel situation to see if you could turn round and make it home, but this is not an option. There are no other islands on your route where you could land to weather out the storm. Your only option is to keep flying. You inform the controllers that this is what you are going to do.

You are beginning to feel the air turbulence as the plane bounces around and you are becoming scared. Very quickly the storm worsens and you know you are going to have the most challenging flight you have ever had. In fact you are beginning to fear for your life. Soon you cannot see where you are going. The plane is dropping as it hits air pockets and dipping from side to side. You can hear the engines labouring as it fights its way into the storm. Instinctively, you close your eyes for a moment and send up a prayer asking for protection and the courage and strength of character to get you through this. Very quickly, the plane is surrounded in a blue haze and the plane appears to have stabilised, even though the storm continues to rage strongly around you.

You get a knowing that you must climb to reduce the impact of the storm and you ask for clearance to do this. Of course this is granted and as you increase altitude you immediately notice the storm becoming less and less. For many minutes the blue haze remains with you. Only when you are on the edge of the storm and the danger has passed does it go away. You know without a doubt that your prayers were answered and that you were protected and given the courage to cope. You also know you were guided to make the right decisions to take the plane out of danger. The sky ahead now shines brightly and you relax and settle in for the rest of your journey reflecting on your experience in the storm. You thank God that you have weathered the storm safely and for your plane having received no damage.

Exercise to ask for protection

1. Look at picture (22) of Archangel Michael.
2. If you are worried about someone in particular place a picture of them on this picture.
3. Call on Archangel Michael to bring them protection, strength and courage.
4. Sit and visualise his blue cloak completely surrounding them, with his sword at the front and shield behind.
5. Say out loud, 'so be it, it is done.'
6. Thank Archangel Michael.

Picture 23 (Chapter 15) – receive an unconscious confirmation that there are angels

A prayer for the angels

1. Look at picture (23).
2. Light a candle and dedicate it to angels.
3. Offer this prayer. 'In the name of God and all that is light, I ask that you give love and light to all the angels that are helping humanity and the universe.'
4. Close your eyes and visualise the heavens glowing with the light of God.
5. Know this to be true.
6. Thank God.

Picture 24 (Chapter 17) – receive help to develop your intuition and higher psychic and spiritual gifts

Meditation – feel the trees

You find yourself in the midst of a tropical jungle. The leaves are wet after a recent downpour and everything smells really strong at the moment. You have a very good guide who you trust completely, which is just as well, as it is riddled with dangerous creatures and vegetation. Each step is enlightening as you discover a new plant, insect or animal you haven't seen before. Your senses are buzzing. After walking for many hours you finally reach the spot where you are to camp for the night. It is a large clearing with small huts high up in the trees. Your guide lights a small fire and its aroma fills the air. It smells sweet. You both sit around the fire.

As the evening starts to close in the sky becomes alive with stars. It is outstanding and the sky has never appeared so beautiful. Your guide starts to chant a repetitive but melodic tune. You join in and you notice your energy start to change. You realise that you are being taken to a higher level and your physical frame no longer registers with your senses. Everything around you now resonates differently. What was a tree is now glorious energy; the fire a different texture and you can no longer 'see' your guide. You realise that you have been joined by angels and taken to a higher place of energy. You are given the privilege of 'feeling' the life of one of the amazing trees in this clearing.

The tree takes you on its journey from being a sapling to the mighty tower it now is. You have a knowing of how the Earth has supported the tree; how the weather has changed it; how animals rely on it; how plants live on it and the many natural disasters that have occurred. The angels keep sharing experiences with you for many hours. Finally, they retreat and your energy slowly returns to its physical state. You are left in awe of what has happened. Your guide helps you safely to your hut in the tree, where you gently fall asleep. When you wake up the next day you know you have had a large shift in consciousness.

Exercise to develop your intuition and higher psychic gifts

This exercise can be completed on your own, but it is much more fun in pairs or as a group.

1. Look at picture (24) of Archangels Jophiel, Metatron, Gabriel, Michael and Lady Nada.
2. Take a pack of playing cards and spread them face down on the floor. Make sure they are really mixed up.
3. Turn up one card and hold the card between your hands.
4. Hold the energy of the card in your heart chakra; place it on the floor face up.
5. Slowly hover one of your hands over the remaining cards. As you do this send out energy from your heart chakra to the archangels asking them to help you 'tune' into the card's partner.
6. Take your time and when your heart senses that you have found the pair to the card you have turned over, take a chance and turn over that card.
7. Do not think about this, let your heart decide
8. As you repeat this exercise you will find this becomes quite easy.
9. You may think this quite trivial for archangels to want to play 'pairs', but quite to the contrary. They deem it a fun way to allow us to connect and trust our hearts.
10. Give your thanks to the archangels.

Picture 25 (Chapter 18) - receive the desire to access your past life wisdom, the protection to do so and the wisdom to use it for your ascension pathway.

Meditation – a visit to a past life

As you sit in your comfortable place, you begin to reflect on your life. You consider what happened last week, last year and in childhood. There has been so much in your life, but you have a strong feeling that there is more. You know somehow that you will find out what this is. With this thought, you become aware of an angel looking at you, inviting you to go with her. You stretch out your hand to her and as she takes your hand, you are enclosed in her energy.

You become acutely aware that your surroundings have changed. You don't know why you know this but you do. You are walking into a past life. She asks you to take all the time you need to explore this life as an observer. You accept this offer knowing you are completely protected and guided. The angel has just one task for you whilst you observe this life. You are asked to find the reason you are being shown it. This reason is relevant to your current life. You accept this willingly. You spend quite a long time to do this.

When you have seen all you need to see of your past life you become aware again of your angel. You tell her what you have found. She asks you to sit down in your comfortable place and listen to what she has to say. She explains to you about the significance of this past life and how 'revisiting' it, has helped you access your past life wisdom. She shares with you how to use it for your ascension pathway. She leaves you with this information and the feeling of being enlightened.

You may wish to try this exercise to connect to other lives you have had.

Receive awareness of your past lives and the capacity to heal them

1. Look at picture (25).
2. Think of a person that seems familiar to you. You may feel comfortable or uncomfortable with them. Alternatively think of a place that you sense you have visited before.
3. Close your eyes and relax.
4. Ask the angels to take you to the past life where you have known that person or been in that place.
5. Sense your angel very close to you, perhaps even holding your hand.
6. In front of you a bridge has appeared and you both start to walk over it.
7. You are walking safely back in time.
8. Count slowly from ten to zero as you go back through the years or centuries.
9. As you step off the bridge find yourself back in the past life. You may have a picture of who you were. You may have a flash or a feeling or a knowing.
10. Ask to receive information about what happened.
11. From the perspective of time, release, forgive and heal all that happened then.
12. Walk back across the bridge to the place you were when you started. You are the same but your consciousness has expanded and a healing has taken place.

Picture 26 (Chapter 18) – receive exhilaration from Source

Exercise to receive exhilaration from Source

1. Look at photograph (26).
2. Feel the energy and know that something amazing is going to occur.
3. Make time to go and watch a sunrise.

4. As you look at it rising, invoke Archangels Christiel, Mallory and Zadkiel to fill your heart with divine energy.
5. Raise your arms to the sky to be thankful for such a wonderful gift.
6. Jump around to consume every bit of this energy.
7. Know that you have been filled with love, light, wisdom and peace.
8. Thank them for this wonderful moment and assure them that you will bring this energy to everyone you meet.

Picture 27 (Chapter 19) – receive energy which propels you to action for the highest good.

Enhance your sense of welcome and belonging on the spiritual path to propel you to action for the highest good.

1. Look at picture (27).
2. Know you are welcomed to your spiritual path to enlightenment.
3. Close your eyes and see a beautiful path up a mountain in front of you. It is lined with trees of so many different colours and it is lit by a violet light.
4. You are surrounded in the energy of Archangel Zadkiel.
5. Everything you see is tinged with love. With every step you take you know you are becoming wiser.
6. As you reach the top of the mountain and look around, you know there is a higher reason for everything.
7. Know that you belong on this path and the spiritual hierarchy is supporting you.

Front cover picture (Chapter 19) - receive a joyous awakening of your heart and your stellar gateway

Meditation –advance your soul on its journey

You find yourself standing in a brilliant but blinding light. It is so bright you have no idea where you are but you know you are completely safe. As your eyes become adjusted to the light you see you are standing on the top of Mount Everest. The view is breathtaking. The sky is blue, the clouds are scattering the horizon below and the air is crisp and fresh. The view begins to change as you become aware of pink blossom trees growing from the clouds and soon everywhere you look, all you can see is pink. The clouds rise up level with the top of the mountain.

You step onto the first cloud and walk knee deep in its essence to the nearest pink blossom tree. As you are standing under the tree it shakes covering you in its blossom. As each piece touches you, you feel your energy expand. You fall to your knees, picking up the petals and you throw them into the air and again they fall on you. This time you begin to notice your heart chakra starting to stir.

You become aware that your chakra is glowing. It is seeking information and this feels good. You do not question why it is asking, it is so normal. You can see the pink energy in the chakra starting to push down through your solar plexus, naval, sacral, base and into the Earth Star chakra. Equally the pink energy flows into the throat, third eye, crown, causal, soul star and stellar gateway chakras.

As the energy connects Earth to the stars you find your heart chakra changes colour to a bright dynamic white and you get a strong knowing that you have just been given information which will progress your soul on its journey. As the energy subsides you notice the pink blossom trees are now covered in white blossom and you feel your heart glow again. You close your eyes and smile, feeling just wonderful. As you open your eyes you find yourself in your home and you realise you have moved further on your path to ascension.

Visualisation to access your stellar gateway

1. Look at the front cover picture
2. Light a candle and find a space where you can be undisturbed.
3. Close your eyes and relax.
4. With your hands in prayer position, invoke the Archangels Mariel, Lavender and Chamuel and know that before you is a staircase reaching so high you cannot see the top. It is golden.
5. Thank them for giving you access to your stellar gateway.
6. You step onto the staircase and with every step up you take, you find you are beginning to glow. The higher you climb the more golden this glow becomes.
7. Enter your stellar gateway.
8. Spend as much time as you wish to sit within its glorious light.
9. Dedicate yourself in service to the divine and ask humbly to be assisted to ensure that all you do is for the highest good.
10. When you have finished climb down the steps, knowing you are now on a new path and that you can return at any time.
11. Thank the archangels for such a wonderful opportunity.

Picture back cover (Chapter 19) – receive an invitation to walk the journey of the heart chakra with Mother Mary's help and a direct link to Mother Mary's heart and the cosmic heart.

Visualisation to join with Mother Mary

1. Look at the picture on the back cover of Mother Mary and Archangel Zadkiel.

2. Light a candle and dedicate it to the highest good.
3. Sit quietly and make sure you will be undisturbed.
4. Visualise Mother Mary's beautiful and vibrant energy enclosing you and holding you in this energy.
5. Breathe in this energy and sense it filling every part of you.
6. Keep within this energy until Mother Mary withdraws this from you.
7. Thank her for this amazing experience.

Picture 28 (Chapter 20) – receive an invitation to the ascension pathway

Meditation – have a positive impact on humanity

Today you are about to land in China. You are very excited as you are to walk the Great Wall of China with other people from around the world. You have this wonderful feeling inside you beginning to form. You know something is about to happen, you just don't know what it is. Finally, you land, pass through customs without a hitch and are transported to meet up with the others. You greet each other with interest. Your group has travelled from across the world to be here. Everyone appears to be very nice. You then check into your hotel for the night. Once this has been done, you all take a walk together to the wall.

You climb to the first tower; it is night now and the stars are twinkling brightly. You form a circle and hold hands as you all want to feel the energy of the wall and those who built it. You begin to chant rhythmically and you bring the sound to a crescendo. The energy running between you is immense and the energy in the centre of the circle so much more. You are aware that surrounding you all is Archangel Metatron's energy, you don't know why you know this, you just do. You cannot see the other side of the circle for the brightness of his light.

As you are held in this light you receive a message which says that 'every step you take must be filled with love and peace for humanity, for it is the little things which mean the most'. The energy remains and you cannot break your hold in the circle. After quite a long time it recedes and everyone slowly steps back from the circle. You each relay your experience and everyone had exactly the same experience. You are very humbled and filled with determination to ensure that every step you take has a positive impact on humanity. You also know that being held in Archangel Metatron's energy has moved your energy to a higher consciousness and that you have experienced a shift on your ascension pathway.

Receive protection from Archangel Michael and guidance from Archangel Metatron

1. Look at picture (28).

2. Invoke Archangel Michael to bring you protection as you walk your pathway to ascension.
3. Invoke Archangel Metatron to guide you on your specific mission for the highest good.
4. Know that your request has been received.

Picture 29 (Chapter 20) – Metatron's cube

Exercise to connect to your higher self through a journey of discovery

1. Look at picture (29).
2. Sit quietly and hold your energy in the highest intention.
3. Ask Archangel Metatron to escort you through the cube.
4. Know you will be guided and protected.
5. Undertake to visit only one area of the cube each time you visit.
6. Keep a journal of your experiences.
7. If any of the experience is unclear then record this and seek clarity by calling on Archangel Gabriel.
8. Undertake this journey slowly and steadily, learning as you go.
9. Each time you undertake this journey thank Archangel Metatron and all those you meet along the way.

Picture 30 (Chapter 20) - receive universal peace in your heart.

Meditation – be a peace maker

'It is with great sorrow that I am here today to give my son to the earth. . .' are the words you hear as you are sitting in a tree near to the cemetery. These are spoken by a lady who has lost her son to war. You climb down from the tree as you feel you are intruding on someone else's grief. You walk away and feel an awful sense of loss. You think to yourself why did this have to happen? Why is war so important?

You decide at that moment to make some positive moves to bring peace to the world. You have no idea what this will be or how you will achieve it; you just know this is what you are going to do. You shout to the universe 'I am a peace maker', and you keep repeating this over and over again. Eventually, exhausted you return to the tree and climb into its branches to rest. The graveyard is at peace now and as you are sitting there you begin to notice that the light around you is getting brighter. Suddenly, you are surrounded by hundreds of angels of love holding you in love. You are comforted and encouraged by this. Gently, the light surrounding you changes from brilliant white to a vibrant gold and you can feel yourself being consumed and held in peace.

You are asked to join the angels and receive information from them, for you are to be an ambassador for peace. You know you can spend as much time as you need to really take on board the detail of the message, so you do. Eventually, the golden light starts to diminish along with the brightness of the white light until you are able to see the tree you are sitting in again. You climb from the tree and jog home to record these messages in your journal. That night as you are just falling asleep, you are met by Archangel Metatron who relays even more information to you. You sleep deeply and in the morning awake ready and determined to bring peace wherever you go. You have recognised that putting energy into stopping something, is actually giving energy to whatever is occurring, so you have opted to give your energy to peace and love.

Exercise to bring forward peace

1. Light a candle and ask Archangel Michael for protection.
2. Close your eyes.
3. Regulate your breathing.
4. Ensure you have a good mix and balance of energy in your solar plexus chakra.
5. Focus on your heart chakra and sense how it feels.
6. Push out the energy from your heart chakra as far as you can.
7. Know with certainty that Archangel Metatron's energy will be felt by your heart chakra.
8. Breathe this energy into your heart chakra.
9. Feel peace being given to you.
10. Ask for clarity to understand if this peace is for you or for you to bring to others.
11. Accept this gift.
12. Draw in your heart chakra energy until it is back to the size it is usually.
13. Thank Archangel Metatron for the gift of peace.

Picture 31 (Chapter 22) – receive a knowing that you are looked after when you die

Exercise to connect with those in spirit.

Remember that life is continuous for yourself and those in spirit. They are just a thought away and the angels bring them to see you.

This exercise may be quite an emotional experience, so please decide if you wish to proceed with it.

1. Look at picture (31).
2. Close your eyes and relax.

3. Hold a picture in your mind of a loved one you wish to connect with.
4. Invoke Archangels Azriel, Raphael, Uriel, Gabriel, Michael, Metatron and Chamuel to hold you in an energy that will allow you to meld with this loved one.
5. Push out your aura until you can feel the emotions of your loved one or until you can see your loved one in front of you.
6. Ask the archangels to bring your loved one into your energy; allowing you to meld with their energy. (This may get quite emotional. If it does you must ask your loved one to move back a bit. They won't mind. Say very firmly 'please stand back a little, I am not quite ready for this much energy at the moment.' Mean it and it will happen. Remember you are in control at all times and that you can just get up and walk away if you wish.)
7. Take all the time you need to say the things that need saying.
8. When you have finished your conversations thank them for coming forward and know that their angels will still bring them to visit you.
9. Close down to ensure you do not have other spirits hoping that you can take a message to another. To do this visualise yourself being completely enclosed in flower as it draws its petals together, a ball of golden light, a room with no windows, a moth cocoon; in fact anything that will make you feel secure and completely encloses you.
10. Cleanse your aura by visualising yourself standing in a waterfall of vibrant blue, with the water drops gently covering you.
11. Thank the archangels for their support and send love and light to the heavens.

Picture 32 (Chapter 25) – receive an invitation to go to El Moyra's etheric retreat

Exercise to visit El Moyra's retreat

1. Look at picture (32).
2. Sit quietly and ask humbly if you can visit El Moyra's retreat.
3. Know that the next time you fall asleep you will visit this retreat.
4. Keep a paper and pencil next to your bed so you can record any memories of the journey as you wake.
5. Know this will occur.

Picture 33 (Chapter 25) – receive a downloading of ancient universal wisdom

Meditation – take a trip to Atlantis
You find yourself zooming through the sky on your dragon. He is holding you gently

in his energy which keeps you safe and steady on his back. You have no idea where he is going and you are not concerned by this. You are just enjoying being with him.

Before you know it you are in a place you have never been before. It is completely different in every way. It is modern yet old, a very different combination. There are people but they are not talking, yet they can communicate. Your dragon lands on the ground and drops his shoulder for you to climb down. You know somehow that you are in Atlantis. You are 'called' to enter a temple, which you do. Here you are held in energy which allows you to communicate with the beings in the temple. Suddenly, you can hear conversation and it is fascinating. As you listen there is no tension, anger, greed or any form of negativity at all. It is outstanding. Before you know it you are assimilating the knowledge being given to you and it is awesome.

You can sense it entering your cells and then responding to the knowledge. In fact you know you are being 'changed' in some way. It is what your body and soul has needed for so long. You cannot move and neither do you want to. You have no idea how long you remain in this energy. Eventually, the energy is pulled back and you are able to see your dragon, bowed ready for you to climb on board. You climb on to his back and his energy now holds you safe again. He soars into the sky at a speed so fast you are unable to make out anything until finally you are delivered safely back to your home.

You know you have so much more now to give to humanity and the universe and this excites you. You sit to reflect on your journey with the knowledge that something amazing has just occurred.

Receive a downloading of ancient universal wisdom

1. Look at picture (33).
2. Close your eyes and feel the energy from Archangels Zadkiel, Raphael, Michael, Gabriel, Uriel and the master Abraham going deep inside you.
3. Know that it is transmuting your life issues and preparing you to receive ancient wisdom.
4. Feel that you are being held up in the light to receive ancient universal wisdom.
5. Breathe in the energy and welcome this download of knowledge.
6. Thank the archangels for allowing you to receive this wisdom.

Picture 34 (Chapter 30) – receive the ability to open your right brain to understand and express wisdom, unconditional love and peace and spread it to the world.

Kathy shares her experience of what it is like to join with Archangels Michael, Gabriel, Uriel, Zadkiel and Mary Magdelene's energy. She has written this as it occurred:

As I look into this Orb I am shown the stars. Instead of seeing the stars as we see them looking up into the night sky, I am looking down on the universe. There is a feeling of excitement and anticipation in the air from the mighty angelic realms. The focus of interest now turns from the stars in general to our planet, Earth. It is holding, very strongly, the wisdom of the Ancients, the intention from the universe and unconditional love. Combined together the energy of the archangels and Mary Magdelene radiate these gifts to those on the Earth plane.

These radiated intentions allow me to connect with the Orb more deeply. I am taken into it, I feel sad initially. I believe what I am interpreting as 'sad' is in fact complete inactivity. It is resting or waiting. It appears like I am 'floating' in space. I have no weight and the space I am in is extremely expansive. Oddly, though, I know where I am in the Orb and I am right in the centre. I have stopped moving and am in a suspended state. Everything is quiet. I know the cells in my body are taken apart one by one.

Each is being examined for impurities and in someway it feels as if I am being reconstructed and yet I am completely peaceful. It is a very strange and yet fascinating experience. I have no idea of time, so I do not know how much time has been given to this. Slowly, I can tell I am being put back together and each reformed cell is full of wisdom. The Orb transforms in front of my eyes. There is suddenly light everywhere and inside it is multi-layered, with what appears to be tunnels running from the central core. The negativity taken from my cells is transmuted and a burst of golden light fills every aspect of the Orb. Instantaneously, it returns to silent and I find I am moving (floating) again. I know I am now protected. Slowly, it withdraws itself from my energy and I am left feeling amazingly refreshed and renewed.

Exercise to open the right side of your brain to understand and express wisdom, unconditional love and peace.

1. Look at picture (34).
2. Think of someone who needs healing and dedicate this exercise to them.
3. Hold a picture in your mind of this person and ask Mary Magdelene to bring forward the healing of the ancients.
4. Know without a doubt that this healing will be just what is needed for both the person and to open the right side of your brain.
5. Thank Mary Magdelene for all she has done for you both.

Picture 35 (Chapter 33) – receive a sense of the vastness of the universe and that you can help humanity ascend

A prayer for humanity

1. Look at picture (35).
2. Light a candle and dedicate it to the universe.
3. Offer this prayer. 'In the name of God and all that is light, I ask that you help humanity ascend so they can sense the vastness of the universe.'
4. Close your eyes and visualise the heavens glowing with the light of God and this light being given to humanity.
5. Know this to be true.
6. Thank God.

Picture 36 (Chapter 35) – receive the courage to go out and make a difference

Meditation - peace

You are really excited as you have been invited to a rally to support peace. You have always had a strong desire to live peacefully and you aspire to bring peace to the world. You are only 11 years and you have found that it has been quite a challenge to support your beliefs in such a material world. You are going with your parents and have packed your rucksack as you are camping in a tent for a couple of nights. You are buzzing with anticipation. However, you are also a little scared as you know that you will get 'picked on' by other children at school. This does worry you as you know they can be cruel.

You set off with your family and a good few hours later you arrive at the rally. There are thousands of people there. Everyone is chilled out and people are mingling together. You can see the reporters hanging around outside waiting to present the news, and even they are mellow. You join others sitting round a large bonfire and someone picks up a guitar and starts to sing. They have a wonderful voice, very melodic, and before long you can feel your energy growing as it soaks in the atmosphere. You sway from side to side to the rhythm of the music and your heart chakra feels so content. Everyone is very peaceful.

The next morning the atmosphere is intense and people are dressed and ready for the march. You have been working for days to make your placard. It is very clear and colourful. It says just one word 'PEACE'. The organiser has asked to meet with the Prime Minister. Just as they are about to be taken into Downing Street, you catch the eye of the Prime Minister, who walks over and asks if you can be allowed to join in the discussions. Your parents permit this, so you follow him into Downing Street. It is very grand. He asks why you are on the march. You explain that you have always had a knowing that peace must return to the world. Eventually, you finish your conversation and are delighted that he wants you to keep in contact by email about your ideas. You are photographed with him on the doorstep of 10 Downing Street.

The next morning your picture is on the front page of every newspaper. You feel very proud. At school the next day, instead of being bullied everyone comes up and talks to you, keen to be your friend. They are now very interested in your views on peace. You are so glad that you followed your heart and you know that you will be able to make a difference now and in the future.

Exercise to go out and make a difference

For this you need a pen and paper. Remember you are a magnificent being and all things are possible with pure intention and angelic assistance.

1. Look at picture (36).
2. Write down 'I want to go out and make a difference.'
3. Ask the Master Rakoczy, Archangels Michael, Uriel, Gabriel and Raphael and unicorns to help you.
4. Know that this will be achieved. Say out loud, 'so be it, it is done.'
5. Look often at this intention and continue to ask the higher beings to enable you to achieve your highest possible spiritual potential.

Picture 37 (Chapter 36) – receive help to use your masculine energy positively and move on to your ascension pathway.

Exercise to use your masculine energy positively

1. Look at picture (37) of the Master Quan Yin and Archangels Michael, Raphael and Zadkiel.
2. Light a candle for all people who have not yet balanced the masculine and feminine aspects of their being.
3. Sit quietly and write down an issue that has been concerning you.
4. Firstly, consider this by only using your mind. How do you feel?
5. Cleanse by drawing a ball of pure blue light up through your body, ensuring it slowly pulls from you all the negativity.
6. Secondly, consider this by drawing the energy of the question into your heart chakra. Allow this energy to permeate through your body. How do you feel?
7. Reflect on these two differing approaches and know that decisions must be made by listening to your heart.
8. Be thankful for this enlightening experience.

Picture 38 (Chapter 37) – receive a knowing that your journey is constantly watched over and assessed.

Ask the angels to support your decisions

1. Look at picture (38).
2. Sit down quietly and tell the angels of your decision, whatever it is.
3. Ask them to support it.
4. Know that, no matter what, your angels are helping you to do what you have chosen.
5. Know that your journey is watched over and that you are assessed and then guided to make the right choices.
6. Move forward with confidence.

Picture 39 (Chapter 38) – receive unconditional love and humility about your role in the divine plan

1. Look at picture (39).
2. Light a candle and dedicate it to humility.
3. Close your eyes and ask St Clare to bring to you the unconditional love and humility that you need.
4. Share your smiles and laughter with each person you meet for the rest of the day.
5. Record their reactions and how this made you feel in a journal.
6. Read your journal often and keep adding to it.
7. Repeat this exercise if your energy levels fall.

Picture 40 (Chapter 39) – receive a total trust in divine connections

Meditation – be happy to be you

You have been preparing for months to get fit. It has been hard but worth it as you have finally reached Machu Picchu. Nothing could have prepared you for the intensity of the feelings you have at this moment. You are exhausted and overwhelmed. This trip has meant so much to you as you are fulfilling your best friend's dream. She couldn't take the trip as she had broken her leg. You sit looking out at the most stunning view with tears rolling down your cheeks. You have no idea how long you stay seated, it just doesn't matter. Eventually, you get up and walk around exploring, taking in the atmosphere. You come across an area which has the most wonderful energy and you stop there.

For some reason you know you have to jump around laughing and shouting, you just can't help it. At that moment you feel very strange. As you look down at your body, you realise you are no longer in your physical body jumping up and down at Machu Picchu, but taken to a place of golden light. Everything is calm and peaceful, including you. You notice that you are now in the presence of a mighty being.

Lord Kuthumi introduces himself as the world teacher and invites you to sit with him, which of course you do. He says he is very humbled to meet with you as you have undertaken a lot to finish what your friend could no longer achieve. This has impressed him greatly. You feel slightly embarrassed for such a great one to be humbled in your presence. He senses this and with his supportive words he helps you to accept who you are. You stay and talk with him for a long time, for he has so much to share with you.

You are held in his golden light throughout this time. Eventually, with your conversation over, you are gently returned to your physical form. By now the night is beginning to draw in and you have to return to your camp. You cannot wait to come back tomorrow as you know you have only just started to build your divine connection and you just want to take this forward more and more.

Exercise to attune to higher frequencies

1. Look at picture (40) of Archangel Faith, Lord Kuthumi and Master Imor.
2. Dedicate a candle to divine connections.
3. Ask Archangel Faith to hold you in the energy you need to keep your connections pure.
4. Ask Lord Kuthumi to open you up to receive the teaching of the universe.
5. Ask Master Imor to give you access to higher wisdom.
6. Know this is given. Say 'So be it, it is done.'
7. Give thanks for this attunement.

Picture 41 (Chapter 41) – receive an invitation to travel intergalactically with Commander Ashtar

Kathy shares her experience of what it is like to join with Commander Ashtar's energy. She has written this as it occurred:

As I enter this Orb I am filled with pride. I am consumed with love and my heart chakra is so expanded I have tears running down my cheeks. It is not because I am sad, it is immense pride I feel and I can't contain it. I know I sense emotions intensely, but there is just an excess of love here. I know that there is a very strong spiritual connection between the beings within this Orb and the child. My head is buzzing with energy. I have energy building up in me and I know that someone wants to speak through me.

I am told that if I enter this Orb further I will be taken out into the galaxy and I am asked if I am ready for this. Of course I say yes. With this decision made, I find I am travelling very fast through what I can only describe as a small flexible tunnel. Everything is a blur. Eventually, the speed slows and I appear to be in a completely different universe. I am not sure what I am look-ing at, I have never seen anything like this ever. I know it is an environment that would support humans but I don't know why I know this. I am conscious that I am not alone and that there is at least one other being with me. I can communicate easily but I cannot see any beings. For some reason this does not seem odd.

I am told that this Orb will be a delight for people who wish to communicate with beings from other planets or for those who desire scientific or spiritual an-swers. I am filled with information before I am transported back to the Orb and to my normal energy. It is now quiet and at rest.

Meditation – to be 'out of this world'.

As night draws in one evening, you and a group of friends go outside, lie down and look at the night sky. It is a warm night and the sky is very clear. You are chatting happily, seeking out all the various constellations and you fall about laughing when someone thinks a plane is a star. During the night you all decide that tomorrow you will travel to Avebury and again spend the night under the stars. The next morning you wake eager to set off.

When you get there it is dusk so you choose a place with a very good feel to it and, unbeknown to you, is on a crossing of the ley lines. There are four of you and you lay down at 90 degrees to each other. Each of you without knowing it has lain exactly on a ley line with your heads converging at the crossing. Tonight as you lay there you feel very different. You sense that you are glowing and that you can be seen from space and this is quite empowering. All the stars look larger and shine brighter. You ask your friends if they also feel the same and they do. You hold hands and immediately the four of you notice everything around you change. Your energy has shifted and you are no longer looking at the stars but are inside what can only be described as a space ship. You all sit up and look at each other with expressions of amazement.

For sitting in front of you is a being not of this world, with the most enfold-ing energy you have ever felt. You know you are somehow part of his energy as you can sense what he is thinking. He does not need to speak to you, you just know. He holds you in his energy long enough for you to ask the many ques-tions you have about other worlds and intergalactic travel. The experience is literally 'out of this world'. Without you realising it you become aware that you are looking at the night sky again and your three friends are next to you. You all sit up in silence looking at each other, knowing that something very profound has just occurred. You travel back to your camp site still in silence, and whilst sitting round the camp fire you begin to slowly and gently share your own ex-periences.

Receive an awakening to higher powers and intergalactic knowledge

1. Look at picture (41).
2. Close your eyes and let the orb resonate in your third eye.
3. Know that you have connected to Commander Ashtar.
4. Feel yourself protected.
5. Sense your higher powers being awakened and ask Commander Ashtar to activate them when you are ready.
6. Thank him and open your eyes.

Picture 42 (Chapter 42) – receive a connection with scientific masters in alignment with the divine plan.

Exercise to enhance your protection and receive an understanding of the awesome knowledge of the scientific masters

1. Look at picture (42).
2. Play a piece of powerful uplifting music.
3. Close your eyes and visualise the deep blue Orb of Archangel Michael protecting you.
4. Picture Archangel Christiel placing a crystal light over you to heighten your listening skills.
5. Ask Master George to help you accept and understand the awesome knowledge you are being given by various scientific masters.
6. Relax and let the knowledge enter your soul.
7. Give thanks for this wonderful opportunity.

Picture 43 (Chapter 43) – receive an expansion of the mind to higher truths

Meditation – to take another opportunity positively

This is a very big day for you at work. You are going to an interview for a job you have wanted for ages. It is promotion and will mean you are able to change your life style completely. If you secure this job you will have much less travelling, but increased responsibility, which suits you fine as you would like to have more time at home with your family. You have prepared well but today you can't remember a thing. In fact as you are trying to get ready to go to work, you find you are in a flap. Your partner is trying to support you, but instead of listening you are snapping and flapping around even more. Eventually, you just collapse in a heap and break down and cry. This is quite out of character as you are usually composed.

It is at this point of complete meltdown you start to listen to your partner, who suggests a warm shower to remove the stress. You accept this happily and as your partner gets the shower warm for you, you ask the universe for support to help you be yourself today. You get into the shower and stand under the falling water. It seems you can feel every drop of water individually and as these land the tension releases from you. The more the tension releases the more you feel confident. You stay in the shower for quite a few minutes, just letting all the stress fall away from you. Eventually, you climb out and you get ready quickly. In fact, it appears that another is telling you exactly what you should do. You are completely confident and chilled out. You give your partner a huge hug to give thanks for bringing you back in focus. You leave for your job interview with quite a skip in your step. You know you look good and your confidence makes you glow. Your mind is completely quiet as you walk to work. Once at work you are able to get on with your work quietly and with ease.

Eventually, you are called for your interview. You close your eyes, take a few deep breaths and smile. As you enter the room your energy enfolds those who are to interview you. You breeze through your interview, with a quiet confidence that seems to infect those questioning you. Whatever, they ask, you take time to assimilate the questions and without thought you have the answers. You have been able to still your mind so you are listening to your guiding angels as they support you to make the right choices for your greater good. You leave the interview knowing that you could do no more. You are very happy with the way you conducted yourself and the answers you gave. You return to work and have the most amazing day, with everyone complimenting you on how wonderful you look today.

For the next few days, when most people are worrying about the interview results, you do not, and you receive a call offering you the position, which you accept happily. You have learned through this experience to relax, free your mind to ask for guidance and know completely that this will be given. You have certainly been enlightened.

Exercise to expand your mind to higher truths

1. Look at picture (43).
2. Light a candle, ask the unicorns to help you clarify your vision and ask the Masters of Orion to bring forward your higher truths.
3. Take a moment to allow this clarity to occur.
4. Thank the unicorns and the Masters of Orion for the help they have given you.

Picture 44 (Chapter 47) – receive the knowing that animals in spirit who love you are with you as you walk you ascension pathway

Meditation – bring peace at night when you sleep

You find yourself as a child about 5 years old. You are a very spiritual child, sensitive and easily scared. You find it very difficult to understand why other children can be cruel to animals and each other. In fact you often chose to play on your own. Your parents are of course a little worried for you as they want you to have lots of friends. You have always seen people in spirit and this has been completely normal for you. For years you have played with many different spirit people. They have been your friends.

For some reason now you are beginning to be scared when you go to sleep as you are being left alone by your spirit friends. You want your friends round you when you go to sleep but they are no longer there at night. So you have started to have nightmares. Your mother, who is very aware of the spiritual activity around you, asks her guide to bring you protection as you sleep. To her joy she is shown a spirit animal which is to be your companion for the rest of your life. The next morning she calls you over to ask you to tell her all about your friends. You are thrilled and spend the next hour telling her all about them. She is delighted that you have been offered so much protection, guidance and wisdom to date. When you have finished telling her all your stories, she says she has got someone very special to be a friend to you for ever. You are very excited and jump up and down, as you can't wait to be told.

Your mother explains very carefully that you have a spirit animal and why it has come to be with you. She ensures you are able to see it clearly by asking you many questions and she makes sure you are able to communicate with this new friend. She asks you to spend as much time as you want to get to know your animal. Eventually, your mother checks with you that you have made friends. You can't wait to tell her all about your animal and again you chat away for ages.

That night, when you go to sleep, you speak with your animal for a little while before dropping into a deep and peaceful sleep. Your parents are of course delighted that you are sleeping again and not having nightmares. At school, the children suddenly all want to play with you. You play sometimes and not others. In fact, you are now so happy your whole energy has changed. You start doing really well in your lessons at school too, as you are now able to listen and are interested in what is being said. You are so pleased that you have a spirit animal that truly loves you and is with you whenever you want. Your smile warms everyone who meets you. Without knowing you have ascended a little.

Exercise to know that animals in spirit love you unconditionally

1. Look at photograph (44).
2. Call on Kulah the tiger to bring forward the animal in spirit which will walk by your side as you progress on your ascension pathway.
3. Feel your heart opening to receive all the love that this creature has.

4. Let the love fill you up from your head to your toes.
5. Thank it for loving you unconditionally.
6. Every time you see an animal send it your unconditional love.

Picture 45 (Chapter 47) – receive the inner peace that enables you to rise above life's challenges

Kathy shares her experience of what it is like to join with Kumeka's energy. She has written this as it occurred:

Kumeka brings a higher consciousness to the human race. He is highly charged with electrons which vibrate extremely fast. The pitch of these vibrations when combined with the Earth's atmosphere brings about the blue tinge within the Orb. They are 'pulled' by the Earth's magnetic forces and this is particularly noticeable when working with ley lines. This is why often Kumeka Orbs appear conical in shape. The energy within is derived from Kumeka's original planet. He has never 'walked' a planet but was assigned a planet to work with. This planet has the highest consciousness and it is here that the first Atlanteans lived. Each of his Orbs brings the essence of this consciousness to us.

It is to bring to light the web of lines that connect our planet to every other planet and to God. As Kumeka and other angels bring about a higher level of consciousness within a person, another light in the Earth's web of light, lights up. The web is partially lit and there is still a lot to do. When Kumeka Orbs are resonating at their highest frequency the Orbs glow 'blue', but inside they are very different. Inside they are bright white light and it is blinding. The energy can enter every aspect of your body and soul and transform your consciousness. As it does this, the bright white light becomes softer and changes to a golden hue full of love. Within the depth of the Orb the Ancient Atlantean consciousness is felt and there is much to learn from here.

Initially, I am not permitted entry to the Orb. Instead it gently holds me in its energy. As this occurs, I feel as if I am watching a film in the making. I am able to walk around the set, but I am not able to be in the film. I know I am in Atlantis. I am 'seeing' only a very small aspect of it, but I know I can return at any time to gather more and more information. I can see the 'temple of light'. It is not a temple as we would know it to be.

The light IS the temple. It is of an extremely strong intensity. It is dense and appears as if it is solid. Many beings have come to be near the temple and to bask in the light. Only the most enlightened are able to enter the light. In fact they meld with it, becoming of it, the temple. It is then that the true messages from God are received. These enlightened ones 'appear' as if they are walking through the temple walls. They then hold this energy, wisdom and knowledge and invite others to come and share it. It is a wonderful sight to see. I try to engage in this sharing and am surprised to find that I am now able to. I immediately find my breathing is symbiotic and I am aware that the embodiment of 'peace' has been downloaded into me. As this occurs the Orb's energy pulls away from me.

Please consider this information before attempting this meditation:

It is essential that you sit quietly and ask Archangel Michael to completely enclose you in his cloak of protection. This meditation is going to start by taking you to a place of low energy and high negativity. This meditation is ideal for people who wish to understand on a deep level how others may be feeling and it will give you the wonderful feeling that can be achieved when these low states are left behind. If you do not feel protected enough, then please do not attempt this meditation.

Meditation – move from negativity to positivity

You are aimlessly walking alone trying to forget everything. You have had the most awful time recently and you have lost your light. Nothing seems to matter and you don't really see or hear anything around you. You begin to notice that something wet is pushing against your hand. You look down and see a dog nudging his nose into your hand. He is quiet and calm and obviously very eager to be with you. You pull your hand away and keep walking. The dog, however, does not give up.

He follows you and again pushes his nose into your hand. You look at him and he has the deepest and most meaningful eyes you have ever seen. He looks right into your soul. He just knows you need to be loved and that you need to accept this love. You sit down and the dog curls up really close to you. After a short while, you bend down and hug the dog. As soon as you do this, you burst into tears. You cry uncontrollably and your sobs are loud as they come from deep within you. You cry for a long time before eventually, you stop. All this time the dog has enfolded you in its energy giving you pure, gentle, unquestioning, unconditional love. You get up and the dog gets up with you. You walk together now and for the first time, for as long as you can remember, you see the flowers.

The dog leads you to touch them and smell their fragrance. With every touch and breath you become lighter. You feel alive. You start to skip and the dog jumps about and starts to run. You can't help yourself you just have to run too. This makes you smile and before long you are laughing out loud. Again, your body shakes, and you are crying, but this time it is tears of happiness. The dog runs to you and puts its nose in your hand and you both fall to the ground in a heap. He smothers you with kisses and you roll about laughing. You know at that moment that everything is alright. You are happy to be you. In fact you are very proud of who you are.

You name the dog 'Hope' as this is what he has given to you. You find people are coming up to you asking if they can stroke him. Of course you say 'yes' as you know how much one touch from a dog can bring to a person. You are astonished and so pleased that the love of an animal could turn your life from darkness to light. You feel free, peaceful and ready to bring happiness to others at every opportunity. As you settle down for the night, with 'Hope' and you thank God for this wonderful encounter and you offer assurance that you will walk in the light and enlighten others wherever you go. You know that tomorrow will bring you so many opportunities and you can't wait.

A prayer to receive inner peace

1. Look at picture (45).
2. Light a candle and dedicate it to inner peace.
3. Offer this prayer. 'In the name of God and all that is light, I ask that you help me achieve inner peace and ensure everything I do is for the highest good.'
4. Close your eyes and know this is done.
5. Give your thanks to God.

Picture 46 (Chapter 47) – receive a knowing of how important the love of animals is for your ascension

Meditation – engage with animals
You find yourself in a very different situation. You have been asked to care for your cousin's small holding while she is away. They have left you with a long list of the things which need to be completed daily. They have horses, pigs, cows, geese, ducks, dogs and cats. You settle in and then take a walk to meet all the animals. Initially, you are daunted and a bit scared of some of the animals. After your initial walk round you sit down to have a cool drink and watch the activity taking place. One of the cats jumps up onto your lap and purrs loudly. It is seeking your attention.

You automatically start to stoke the cat and can feel immediately the tension fall from you. In fact you sense a whole energy rebalance occur. You know that you must connect which each of the animals, as in turn they will offer healing to help you rise above life's challenges. You have never quite understood why your cousin would want so many animals, until now. You get up and thank the cat for enlightening you. The geese and ducks are swimming happily on their pond. Some are sleeping on the bank. They have no desire to be busy instead they feel immensely free. You know that these animals will help you rethink your life to help you approach things differently in future.

The pigs love to be massaged, whether this is by you stroking them or by wallowing in the mud. They don't care, they just know that a massage and contact with the earth and others is very healing for the soul. The cows have a knowing that they are gentle giants and that by going about their business quietly and sensitively they can bring peace to those who watch them. The horses are powerful, graceful and strong. They know they offer the opportunity for people to understand these qualities and that they can teach them to use these for the greater good. They will not be pushed around. The dogs are true companions. You can sense that they want to be with you, that they are guarding you and above all they want to please you. You know that what you thought was going to be quite a stressful time for you is going to be one of the most enjoyable and enlightening experiences you have had to date. You take what these animals have to offer you and bask in the energy many times a day.

You are happy to be guided and to know that everything you are given will stay within your energy. You are confident that you have raised your consciousness to a higher level. You are extremely grateful for this wonderful opportunity and thank the universe for everything you are giving and receiving.

Exercise to know how important the love of animals is for your ascension

1. Look at picture (46).
2. Find a place where you can be quiet and undisturbed.
3. Light a candle and dedicate it to the love of animals.
4. Close your eyes and breathe comfortably until you feel relaxed.
5. Many animals are coming to be with you, all bringing love and peace. They know how important it is for you to receive and give love unconditionally.
6. When they have finished giving love and peace to you, you in turn ooze love and give this back in return.
7. Thank all those who came to you.
8. Open your eyes and notice how your heart feels.

Picture 47 (Chapter 48) – receive an invitation to go to the Great Pyramid to access information for your ascension journey

Meditation – recognise who you are
You find yourself in the middle of a great chamber. This has been cut into the side of a mountain high up out of the reach of many and you have walked for days to reach it. Inside it is magnificent. The walls are strewn with crystals each radiating its own light. In the centre of the chamber is a huge crystal. What is very interest-

ing is that it is not a crystal known to man. It is turquoise and green. It is clear one minute and cloudy the next. You are completely fascinated with it. As you get close you enter its energy and you immediately know that it is still liquid in the centre. You sit with your back against this crystal with your eyes closed and are consumed with its energy.

In fact it feels as if you are within it. You find you are bathed one second in pure white light with your chakras becoming expanded, the next you are within a waterfall and each water drop is bringing purification. Then you are in a fire. It does not burn you but removes all negative energies from you. As you open your eyes you are no longer in the chamber but at the Great Pyramid and gathered there are many ancients from Lemuria and Atlantis and also the great Egyptians. They have been expecting you and preparing you for this meeting today. They say it is time for you to recognise who you are.

Each in turn, encloses you in their energy, offers you healing and opens you up to receive their wisdom. This continues for many hours until each has given you what you need. It is then that you notice things which you have never been able to see before. Words and symbols are moving around in the ether and you know that you can access these at any time by just visualising and asking for their support. With this realisation they are content that you are now connected to your true self so one by one they leave.

You are left sitting cross legged on the floor. You close your eyes and when you open them you are still resting against this crystal. The crystal is pulsing light into the chamber for you to see. You stand up and thank the crystal for offering you the support needed to make your connection with the ancients. With that, you leave the chamber and make your way back to your home. You know without a doubt that something very profound has occurred today and that you are connected to information to help you on your ascension pathway.

Visualisation to visit the Great Pyramid

1. Look at picture (47) of Archangels Zadkiel and Christiel.
2. Sit quietly and hold the vision of the ankh in your mind.
3. Feel the energy of the ankh surround you. You are surrounded by light. How does this feel?
4. As you are held in this energy allow Archangels Zadkiel and Christiel to bring forward information from the ancients of Lemuria, Atlantis and Egypt.
5. Ask for support to be open to receive this.
6. Know that this will be done.
7. Quietly and with peace in your heart thank all those who have made this happen.

Picture 48 (Chapter 48) – receive a sense of the grace of the universe

Meditation – what an angelic display!

You find yourself sitting at the edge of a cliff. It is extremely high yet you do not feel you will fall. You are looking out across the vast expanse of the American outback and the view is amazing. You feel at that moment, such peace. You have a knowing that you are completely safe so you decide to meditate. You close your eyes and regulate your breathing. You begin to hum quietly and slowly you bring this to a chant and a crescendo and then steadily you return to silence. This you do for ten minutes and as you do this you feel quite a shift in your energy.

On completion of your meditation you open your eyes and are struck by the most awesome sight. The sky is full of angels. In fact, everywhere you look there are angels. You know that something amazing must be occurring. To your complete astonishment the angels, in unison, combine their energy. The sky turns into a colourful show of energy. The Northern Lights have nothing on this. It feels as if there is an angelic celebration occurring and you are observing this. The sky keeps changing just like a kaleidoscope and you are completely enthralled.

One by one the angels break from this array and gently tend to a buffalo or move to some other business. One comes forward and holds you in its energy. You find you are now with the angel in flight and you are within the activity the angels are undertaking. It is breathtaking. You are shown that the Earth's web of light is getting brighter too. This gives you the most amazing sensation and you know that you must continue to work alongside the angels bringing light to all you meet. You also feel how happy the Earth is as its lights become bright again. Gently, the angel returns you to the cliff edge and slowly one by one the angels raise their energy to that of the 7th dimension, so you can no longer physically see their energy and the sky returns to its vibrant, pure and cleansing blue. This has been a sensational experience, one you will never forget. With this thought in mind, you get up to walk away, fulfilled and at peace.

Invoke an angel of love

An invocation is a very powerful way of drawing the forces of the universe in to help you. Put your heart and soul into your request.

1. Look at picture (48).
2. Light a candle and dedicate it to the grace of the universe.
3. Say aloud or in your head, 'In the name of God I now invoke an angel of love to come to me.'
4. Trust that one has responded and is with you.
5. Pause and allow yourself to feel its light and love enfold you.

6. Let the love enter every cell of your body and give this up willingly to the universe.
7. Know that the seraphim will accept your love with grace.
8. Know that the universe will respond accordingly.
9. Thank all who have allowed you to walk a few more steps on your pathway to ascension.

As I am sitting here considering how to finish this part of our book I am consumed with emotions. I want to cry. I can feel how excited the angelic hierarchy is. How proud they are. They are truly impressed that we (not just Diana and I, but everyone) have been able to capture the Orbs on our cameras and that now we have an opportunity to really connect with them on a soul level.

They are keen to say that the Orbs are their way of opening their windows for us. They so want us to connect with them and to benefit from all they can give. I just can't describe how I feel right now. I am so very humbled to be a part of this. With this in mind, I give you love, light, peace and grace to support you on your continued pathways to ascension.

How to recognize Orbs

Each of the Orbs has a signature which can be recognised. However, spirit frequently reminded us to explore them with our hearts not our intellect. Let your intuition tell you who they are.

Generally the nearer an Orb is to you the fainter and bigger it is. For example a distant unicorn is a very bright, small dot, while one who is enfolding you is huge and pale.

The Orbs are all of the angelic hierarchy. The elementals and angels always conduct and protect the spirits of people and animals who have been incarnated on Earth.

Ghosts

These are the spirits of those who have not passed into the light and are stuck in the Earth plane. Each is accompanied by an elemental known as a wuryl. These are usually small, faint, white Orbs without a bright or defined border. They sometimes gather in portals where the energy is lighter and they can receive assistance to pass.

Angels carrying spirits

In our experience these are the most prolific and common of all Orbs. The spirits are people or animals who have passed into the light. When they travel they are accompanied by an angel, which is the Orb. The Orbs can be tiny or large and are invariably present at celebrations because loved ones in spirit want to witness the event. Small ones appear to have a small darker dot within a white circle and are often very close to people or animals.

Larger ones are also white with a defined edge and the face or faces of the spirits being carried often appear as a darker mark within the Orb. Sometimes the face can be clearly seen and on occasion are recognised by the person they have come to visit.

You can differentiate these from elementals carrying ghosts because the angels are a visible ring round the outside edge.

Very often the angel bringing the spirit will merge with some of Archangel Michael's protective energy so that blue can be discerned in the Orb.

Archangels carrying Masters

When masters, who have at any time incarnated on Earth travel, they are accompanied by one or more archangels to protect them and hold their energy while they deliver their message. The only exception to this is when a master travels within the golden Christ Light, which is totally protective. When you enlarge one of these Orbs you can often see the master's face quite clearly.

Guardian Angels

These are usually milky white discs, defined but often small and faint. The more help an individual needs, for example if they are feeling uncomfortable in a situation, the closer and larger the Orb will be. They are sometimes seen over a person's ear, talking to them, or over the third eye, protecting them from seeing something psychically or enabling them to see situations or relationships differently.

Angels of Protection

These are milky white discs, similar to guardian angel Orbs but generally larger. They are sometimes seen on the walls of a room that needs to be cleansed, such as a hotel where people of different energies have been using the space. Huge cloudy white Orbs of protection can be seen on houses or forms of transport, holding the energy safely.

Other angels

There are angels of joy, transmutation, peace, happiness, celebration, commitment and many others which look similar to guardian angels; milky white discs. Usually the location will indicate which angel energy they carry. For example, if a room is being renovated you will find angels of transmutation. If there is a celebration you may see angels of joy.

Angels of Love

You can easily recognise these because of their glowing white light. They appear as the brightest of the angels. When an angel of love is witnessing what is happening it is a round white light but as soon as it starts to move you can see its trail. Tiny ones can look like tadpoles while large ones appear as huge rockets. When they zoom round people or animals bringing healing, love and light, they often look like long thin streaks of white light.

These white streaks can merge together into unusual shapes, like flowers or many heads coming from a central ball. They are often oval shaped as they actively radiate healing or protection to elementals, spirits or masters.

They frequently merge with angel or archangel Orbs and make them appear luminous. They also accompany archangel Orbs as an act of loving service.

Elemental Orbs

Fairies
Fairies look like tiny white pinpricks of light and are often seen in clusters.

Esaks
Esak Orbs are smaller than fairies and often appear as tiny white flakes, found where there has been psychic or physical negativity to clear.

Kyhils
As esaks but they are seen in water.

Imps, elves, and gnomes
These are very rarely seen but are very tiny pinpricks of light.

Pixies
Pixie Orbs look like tiny white circles.

Archangel Orbs

Archangels each work on a colour ray and carry that vibration. The archangel itself is a deep intense colour, while their angels are a lighter shade as they carry less of the energy. The more archangel energy there is in an Orb the deeper and purer the colour.

Some of the archangels also have distinctive patterns. Where archangel energy has merged with another Orb you can usually distinguish the colours or defining patterns.

Archangel Azriel (angel of birth and death)
Archangel Azriel is a shining black.

Archangel Butyalil (looks after cosmic energy round Earth)
Archangel Butyalil is pure white. The chambers within it sometimes look square or oval.

Archangel Chamuel (love)

Archangel Chamuel is a beautiful soft pink as it heals hearts.

Archangel Fhelyai (animals)

Archangel Fhelyai is a golden colour between that of Archangels Uriel and Jophiel. It can be recognised by the ring round the outside for he is contained in pure Source energy. He is also slightly opaque because his energy is so strong that animals need to be protected from the strength of his light.

Archangel Gabriel (purity)

Archangel Gabriel shimmers pure white and distinctive concentric circles can be seen within the Orb.

Archangel Gersisa (looks after the leylines)

Archangel Gersisa is seen as grey. It is an oval shape and at the full moon this shape is extenuated. At the full moon it becomes oval and you can see the ley lines on which it is working, coming to a central point within it.

Archangel Jophiel (wisdom through the crown)

Archangel Jophiel's colour is a pale yellow.

Archangel Metatron (wisdom and ascension)

Archangel Metatron, the mightiest of the archangels, in charge of the stellar gateway, radiates deep gold, through orange and sometimes red.

Archangel Michael (protection and strength)

Archangel Michael is a deep blue. His energy is often seen surrounding other Orbs if he is protecting the being they are carrying or he may be sending protection to a person or place.

Archangel Purlimiek (nature)

Archangel Purlimiek appears as a translucent pale green white.

Archangel Raphael (healing and abundance)

Archangel Raphael is bright emerald green and has concentric circles within his Orb as he radiates healing and abundance.

Archangel Roquiel (Connection with Mother Earth)

This universal Earth angel is black. He is often seen with Archangel Sandalphon.

Archangel Sandalphon (Earth Star)

Archangel Sandalphon is black and white but often appears as grey.

Archangel Uriel (confidence and peace)

Archangel Uriel is deep yellow. If he has been collecting negativity which he has not yet transmuted into light, he can appear brown. You can see the chambers within his Orb which are raised like little rounded pearls. If you cannot see his yellow gold colour you will recognise the shapes.

Archangel Zadkiel (transmutation)

Archangel Zadkiel can be distinguished by his lovely translucent violet light of transmutation.

Seraphim

You can recognise the seraphim by their translucent quality. They are usually alone and shimmer with many pastel colours, predominantly blue.

Unicorns

As with the other Orbs the nearer a unicorn Orb is to you, the bigger and paler is their pure white light. Distant unicorn Orbs are like very bright dots in the sky, much clearer than stars. When they are very close to someone's physical body they are large and a diffuse soft white, unless actively engaged, when they become transparent.

Unicorn Orbs a few feet from a person can be recognised by the distinct white swirling pattern within them.

Transparent Orbs

An Orb becomes transparent if the angel is holding the energy while the person is waiting to respond. I have a picture of my granddaughter running about a play park in high excitement totally oblivious of danger. The guardian angel Orb over her is huge and transparent as it holds the energy while she has the opportunity to assess the situation.

Shapes of Orbs

Round

When an Orb is round it is witnessing a situation and holding the energy for the highest outcome.

Straight sided or concave

An Orb changes shape if it is actively sending out protection or transmitting a particular energy or information. One or all sides may become straight or concave depending on how much it needs to radiate.

Hexagonal

When all six sides of an Orb become straight, so that it is a hexagon, it is fully operational. This can be seen in any type of Orb.

Elongated

Orbs which are moving fast can appear elongated or thin and snakelike. They may have a tail or leave a trail behind them.

Conical or lemon shaped

These are Orbs which are receiving energy directly from the sun or an archangel.

Merged Orbs

When several angels merge together their colours or qualities may be represented within the Orb. If they want to keep their qualities separate their colours will appear in blocks within the Orb.

Glossary

Abraham – Lord of Karma of the 10th Ray.

Akashic records – The karmic records of every thought, word and deed of humanity.

Amma, Mother – An avatar or divine incarnation who lives in Kerala, India.

Angels – Angels are spiritual beings who come from the heart of God and vibrate at the seventh dimension. They have no free will and evolve by their service to the divine.

Ankh – Egyptian symbol for life and immortality.

Archangels – Higher angels who are in charge of the angels. There are thousands of them, though only a few who work with humans.

Archangel Amethyst –Twin flame and feminine counterpart of Archangel Zadkiel.

Archangel Aurora –Twin flame and feminine counterpart of Archangel Uriel.

Archangel Azriel –The angel of birth and death.

Archangel Butyalil –A universal angel who keeps the vast currents of the Universe that affect our planet in order. In order to do this he works with Archangel Purlimiek and the nature kingdoms and Archangel Gersisa and the earth kingdoms. He communicates with archangels on other planets. The unicorns are also assisting him with his task, as is Archangel Metatron.

Archangel Chamuel –The angel of the heart who resonates with the pink of love. He brings love, compassion and helps people find forgiveness. Where there is pink in an Orb, Archangel Chamuel's energy is there.

Archangel Charity –Twin flame and feminine counterpart of Archangel Chamuel.

Archangel Christine –Twin flame and feminine counterpart of Archangel Jophiel.

Archangel Faith –Twin flame and feminine counterpart of Archangel Michael.

Archangel Fhelyai (pronounced Felyay) –Works with animals on Earth and on the other side.

Archangel Gabriel –Appears as pure white. He brings purification, joy and clarity. So if you look into one of his radiant Orbs you will receive those qualities in your life.

Archangel Gersisa – A feminine energy this angel helps Archangels Sandalphon and Roquiel with the clearance of the Earth Star chakras of humanity and keeps the leylines clear.

Archangel Hope –Twin flame and feminine counterpart of Archangel Gabriel.

Archangel Jophiel –Works with the vibration of golden yellow, and brings you wisdom and illumination. He is in charge of the development of the crown chakra.

Archangel Joules – Twin flame of Archangel Roquiel, in charge of the oceans.

Archangel Lavender –Twin flame and feminine counterpart of Archangel Mariel, of the soul star chakra.

Archangel Mallory –Twin flame and feminine counterpart of Archangel Christiel.

Mary –Known as Mother Mary. Twin flame of Archangel Raphael. A universal angel of the highest order.

Archangel Metatron – In charge of the Stellar Gateway chakra, which connects us to Source. He works with the Great Pyramid and supervises the karmic records. Twin flame of Archangel Sandalphon.

Archangel Michael – Works with the blue ray offering protection, strength and courage.

Archangel Purlimiek –The angel in charge of nature. He works with the cosmic archangels as well as those of the inner Earth. It is he who gives different elementals their various tasks to do.

Archangel Raphael – The angel of healing and abundance. He works on the emerald green ray and helps to open up the third eye.

Archangel Roquiel – A universal angel who works deep in the Earth helping Lady Gaia. His twin flame Archangel Joules is in charge of the oceans of the world.

Archangel Sammael – He clears and prepares the way for those who Archangel Metatron puts forward to connect with Seraphina.

Archangel Sandalphon –The twin of Archangel Metatron, working with the Earth Star chakra. He carries prayers to God.

Archangel Uriel – The angel of peace and wisdom, who dissolves fears. He gives confidence and serenity.

Archangel Zadkiel – Oversees the Angels of Transmutation who work with the Violet Flame. He also aligns closely with St. Germain and he prepares the Soul Star Chakra for its higher work.

Ascended Masters – Beings who have mastered the lessons of their planets and ascended. Many of these act as teachers in the inner planes.

Ashtar, Commander – The commander of the intergalactic fleet of space ships stationed round Earth.

Babaji –An ascended master known as the deathless avatar.

Bahjans – Sanskrit chants.

Blavatski, Madam – Initiator of the Theosophical Society.

Catherine, St. of Sienna. Lord of Karma for the 12th Ray. Stimulates the spiritual light within humanity.

Clare, St. – Ascended Master of the Higher Hierarchy bringing spiritual awareness to humanity..

Dom – The elemental master of the air elementals.

Dwjhal Kuhl – Ascended Master, deputy to Lord Kuthumi, known as Messenger to the Masters and Hierophant of the Brotherhood of the Golden Robe.

Elementals – Nature spirits, who may belong to fire, air, earth, water or wood. They look after all the different aspects of the natural world.

Air elementals – beings who only contain the element air. These include fairies, Esaks and sylphs.

Earth Elementals – beings who only contain the element earth, including pixies, elves and gnomes.

Water elementals – beings who only contain the element water: mermaids, kyhils and undines.

Fire elementals – beings who only contain the element fire. These include salamanders

Combined elements – imps, dragons and fauns.

El Morya – Master of the first Ray. Helping us with the changes ahead and opportunities for ascension. He is a member of the White brotherhood and originates from Mercury.

Elohim – Creator Angels.

Elohim – Vista, Lord of Karma for the fifth ray.

Elves – Earth elementals who work with trees.

Enoch – Ascended Master who keeps the akashic records of the Jewish race.

Esaks – New to this planet. They have arrived to help us and also to learn about Earth and life here. They act like vacuum cleaners, sucking up negative energy.

Fairies – Nature spirits, about 1ft or 30cms tall, who belong to the element air and look after flowers. They are mischievous, fun loving, pure and innocent. They work with angels and unicorns and there are angels in charge of groups of fairies.

Fauns –Elementals of earth, air and water who help to balance the energy of forests through photosynthesis.

Gandhi –An ascended master of peace recently incarnated in India, known as the Mahatma or Great Soul.

Gautama, Lord Buddha, Master of the tenth ray.

Gaya, Lady – A throne, a very high angel, in charge of Earth and often known as Mother Earth.

Gayatri mantra. The most protective and illuminating of the Sanskrit chants – Om Bhur Bhuvah Svah Tat Savitur Varenyam Bhargo Devasya Dhimahi Dhiyo

Yonah Prachodayat.

George, Master – Kathy Crosswell's brother and newly ascended master.

Germain, St. – Now the Keeper of the Golden Scales.

Ghosts – The spirits of those who are earthbound after leaving their bodies. They are not alone, for an elemental called a wuryl is assigned to hold them until they see the light. In this book we refer to ghosts as spirits.

Gnomes – Shy and sturdy earth elementals who work with the deeper layers of soil and rocks.

Goblins – Earth elementals.

Goddess of Liberty – Lord of Karma for the second ray.

Great Divine Director – Lord of Karma for the first ray.

Guardian angels – Guardian angels are the lowest of the angelic hierarchy. One is assigned to look after every human. They evolve with their charges.

Hilarion – Master of the fifth ray.

Horus – Egyptian god. Immaculate conception by Isis.

Imor – Ascended Master working with Archangel Jophiel to bring in wisdom.

Imps – Tiny elementals 1″ or 2.5cms tall. They are of the combined elements earth, air and water. They aerate the soil and help seeds grow. They work with the pixies.

Isis – Egyptian Goddess, High Priestess in Atlantis, incarnation as Mary.

Jeshua Ben Joseph – The man who attained the name Jesus.

Jesus – The great being who brought in the Christ light for humanity. Known as Sananda in the inner planes and working beside Lord Meitreya as Overlord for the planet.

Josiah – Lord of Karma of the eighth ray.

Karma, Lords of – Higher angels in charge of the karma of individuals and the planet.

Kumeka – Lord of Light - Master of the Eighth Ray. He has never incarnated on Earth but is from another universe where he ascended. Earth has now earned the right to have his presence. His task is to transmute the old and bring enlightenment.

Kuthumi – The World Teacher and head of the Schools of Learning.

Kyhils – Tiny water elementals who hoover up negative energy in the waters of the world.

Lanto – Chinese philosopher and Master of the second ray.

Lemuria –A great civilization prior to Atlantis.

Lone Wolf – Ascended Master and Native American Indian spirit guide.

Ma Ra – Lemurian incarnation of Mary.

Mary Magdelene – Master of the fifth ray

Melchior – Incarnation of El Morya and one of the three Wise Men.

Melchizedek – Head of the Melchizedek priesthood.

Meitreya – Lord of the World, responsible for the entire solar system. Head of the White Brotherhood and Order of Melchizedek. He overlit Jesus and Krishna during their incarnations.

Mermaids – Elementals who are well known and loved for they work with the flora and fauna of the oceans.

Monad – Your original divine spark from God.

Nada – Lord of Karma for 3rd Ray and Master of 7th ray.

Neptune – The elemental master of the water elementals.

Orion, Masters of – The Wise Ones of Orion.

Pallas Athena – Goddess of Truth – Lord of Karma for 4th Ray.

Paul the Venetian – Master of the third ray.

Peter the Great – Lord of Karma for the eleventh ray.

Pixies – Earth elementals who look after the structure of soil, trying to help stop soil erosion. They also work with the bees to help get flowers pollinated.

Portia, Lady – Lord of Karma for seventh ray. Goddess of Justice.

Poseidon – Greek god, High Priest of Atlantis, strategist of the nature kingdom.

Powers – High ranking angels which include the Lords of Karma, Angels of Birth and Death.

Quan Yin, Goddess of Mercy, Lord of Karma for the sixth ray. Master of the twelfth ray.

Rakoczy – Master of the eleventh ray.

St. Germain – Formerly Lord of Civilization. Now the Keeper of the Golden Scales.

Salamanders – These elementals work with fire and respond to the emotions of humans.

Seraphim – The highest of the angelic hierarchy. They maintain the vibration of God's creation.

Serapis Bey – Master of the fourth ray.

Source – The Creator, God.

Spirit Guides – These are the spirits of those who have passed over and gone through training in the inner planes to guide humans. You may have several, all of whom are helping you with different aspects of your life.

Spirits – These are the spirits of those who have passed over who often continue to visit you, watch over you and join you for celebrations and times of mourning. They also travel to continue their own training in the inner planes.

Sylphs – Tiny air spirits who work with flowers and plants to enable the light of the sun to enter the leaves They help to keep the air round flowers and plants pure so that they can live in clear energy. They also assist the flight of birds.

Theresa of Avila, St. – An ascended master of the Higher Hierarchy bringing Oneness to religions.

Thor – Master of the fire elementals.

Thoth Hermes – Priest avatar in Golden Atlantis and Egyptian god.

Undines – Water elementals who help to keep the waters of the world in divine right order.

Unicorns – Ascended horses of the 7th dimension, bring enlightenment, purity and love to places and individuals. They are of the angelic hierarchy and work with people who have a vision which will help others.

Voosloo – Master of the ninth ray.

Vuyamus – Higher self of Sanat Kumara, the Planetary Logos.

Wuryls – Elementals assigned to help and hold all stuck souls who have not passed into the light.

Wywyvsil – Kathy Crosswell's guide. A Lord of Light who has never incarnated on Earth. He is from another universe and has recently arrived here to help our planet. He is a power, a Lord of Karma and Angel of Birth.

See *New Light on Ascension* by Diana Cooper for more information about the Masters who are currently serving in the spiritual hierarchy.

Bibliography

Cooper, Diana : *Discover Atlantis*, Hodder Mobius, (UK) London, 2005 / Findhorn Press, Scotland, 2007 (USA)

New Light On Ascension, Findhorn Press, Scotland, 2004

The Web of Light, Hodder Mobius, London, 2004

The Wonder of Unicorns, Findhorn Press, Scotland, 2008.

Crosswell, Kathy, Cooper Diana, *Enlightenment Through Orbs*, Findhorn Press, Scotland, 2008

Websites:

www.dianacooper.com

Alison Chester-Lambert. www.midlandsschoolofastrology.co.uk

www.kathycrossswell.com

Diana Cooper and Kathy Crosswell take you on an inner journey, gently but firmly guiding you through four 15-minute meditations each (8 in total), asking you to focus each time on a color photograph of an Orb in the accompanying booklet.

1. Journey to meet an angel of love to fill your heart with joy, compassion, happiness and love and then Archangel Chamuel will connect you to the cosmic heart.

2. Blue Orb meditation with Archangels Michael and Uriel, with a unicorn and the Master El Morya.

3. Receive a boost on your ascension pathway (Orb of Archangels Uriel, Michael, Metatron, Gabriel and Raphael, with Serapis Bey, Paul the Venetian, Lord Meitreya, Mother Mary and spirits).

4. Visit the Great Pyramid so that you can bring forward information from the ancient civilizations of Egypt, Atlantis and Lemuria to assist your ascension pathway.

5. Share in the light and bring forward information from Wywyvsil and Archangel Raphael.

6. Access the light of Archangel Faith, Lord Kuthumi and the Master Imor, to bring you information and opportunity to receive a total trust in your divine connection.

7. Access the light of Archangels Zadkiel, Raphael, Michael, Gabriel, Uriel and the Master Abraham, to bring you information and opportunity to receive a downloading of ancient universal wisdom.

8. Access the light of Archangels Mallory, Uriel and Michael to receive the desire to access your past life wisdom, the protection to do so and the wisdom to use it for your ascension pathway.

Double CD ISBN 978-1-84409-155-3

***

This book is an introduction and initiation to the phenomenon of orbs and can be used as an experiential tool by everyone.

World renowned author Diana Cooper and spiritual teacher Kathy Crosswell have examined thousands of photographs containing them, and in this book they explain what the orbs are, their purpose and how they can help you. They answer technical questions and offer practical guidance.

Paperback ISBN 978-1-84409-153-9

FINDHORN PRESS

Life-Changing Books

For a complete catalogue,
please contact:

Findhorn Press Ltd
117-121 High Street
Forres IV36 1AB
Scotland, UK

t +44(0)1309 690582
f +44(0)131 777 2711
e info@findhornpress.com

or consult our catalogue online
(with secure ordering facility) on

www.findhornpress.com

For information on the Findhorn Foundation Community:

www.findhorn.org